Your Love
Horoscope
2004

Your Love
Horoscope
2004

Your Essential Astrological
Guide to Romance and Relationships

Sarah Bartlett

Element
An Imprint of HarperCollins*Publishers*
77–85 Fulham Palace Road,
Hammersmith, London W6 8JB

The website address is:
www.thorsonselement.com

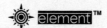

and *Element* are trademarks of
HarperCollins*Publishers* Ltd

First published by Element 2003

1 3 5 7 9 10 8 6 4 2

A catalogue record of this book
is available from the British Library

ISBN 0 00 714398 2

Printed and bound in Great Britain by
Clays Ltd, St Ives plc

To P.

Contents

Introduction

Astrology is about how we are, not why we are.

Your Sun sign offers you the chance to understand more about love relationships that occur in your life and how you deal with them. Through becoming more aware of who you are, you can begin to understand what kind of patterns and experiences you are likely to encounter in the future, and also discover how to deal with your own rhythms and cycles of feelings, emotions and moods. Knowing what to expect from yourself and your relationships prepares you for the wonderful highs and the inevitable lows of romance, emotion and sexual desire.

This book not only guides you astrologically through 2004 with a month-by-month forecast, but also reveals with whom you're compatible and who might pose a few problems, both in bed and out of it. Enjoy.

Astrology Key Words

What is Sun-sign Astrology?

Popular astrology describes the effects that the other planets have in relation to your Sun sign, and subsequently their influence on your destiny, as they move through the zodiac during the year.

The Movement of the Planets

The planets appear to move through the sky against the backdrop of the zodiac. And similarly, they seem to move through your horoscope, which is a snapshot of the sky at the time when you were born. As they move, they sometimes appear to accelerate or they slow down and almost seem to stop altogether. Planets like Mars and Mercury often seem to 'surge' forward into the next sign and slower ones, like Saturn, almost lumber. All planets except the Sun and the Moon can also appear to move backwards, which is called retrograde motion. I use terms like 'backtracking' or 'doing a U-turn' or 'turning turtle' to describe this motion. The effects are usually to slow down events and give you time to reflect on issues. But Mercury retrograde, for example, also signifies delays, hiccups, machinery breaking down or plans getting delayed.

The Planets Are ...

The Sun   The Sun takes approximately one month to move through each sign of the zodiac. It influences your personal destiny, love goals and aims.

The Moon   Taking only a few days to move through one sign of the zodiac, the Moon's cycle effects your emotional reactions, needs and feelings on a daily basis.

Mercury   Fast moving but erratic, Mercury effects your communication throughout the year and the way you interact with lovers and friends.

Venus   Venus influences your eye for beauty, pleasure and sexual happiness, and the kind of people who are drawn to you. Throughout the year it energizes your attraction factor and your charisma.

Mars   Mars effects your sexual desire, how you go after what you want and how you get it, but it also makes you angry and reveals how you confront experiences and relationship issues.

Saturn   Saturn influences structure and boundaries in relationships. But it also brings you back down to earth with a bump if you've overshot the mark.

Jupiter   Often called the planet of 'luck', Jupiter brings adventure, risks, high romance and excitement to your love life.

Uranus   Unpredictable and radical, Uranus brings sudden events and surprise meetings, and is often the catalyst for that electrifying chemistry between strangers.

Neptune   Dreamy Neptune casts a romantic glow over everything, but also glamorizes people and events, and sometimes confuses you about your true feelings.

Pluto   Transformative Pluto influences your deepest emotions, your sexual passion and triggers off the greatest changes in your relationships, for good and bad.

Ruling Planets

The planet which rules your Sun sign is very important because it adds another flavour to your Solar journey. Every sign of the zodiac has a 'ruler' or a planet which is the henchman for your Sun:

Aries is ruled by Mars
Taurus is ruled by Venus
Gemini is ruled by Mercury
Cancer is ruled by the Moon
Leo is ruled by the Sun
Virgo is ruled by Mercury
Libra is ruled by Venus
Scorpio is ruled by Pluto
Sagittarius is ruled by Jupiter
Capricorn is ruled by Saturn
Aquarius is ruled by Uranus
Pisces is ruled by Neptune

Aspects

Aspects occur when there is a resonant dynamic played out between two planets in the sky and in your horoscope. It appears as if they form an angle and the most important ones are called trines (120 degrees apart), squares (90 degrees apart), conjunctions (when they appear to be in the same degree), sextiles (60 degrees apart) and oppositions (180 degrees apart). Aspects to your Sun add a very powerful combination of the energy or characteristics of the planets involved in the aspect.

Zones

These are areas of the Sun-sign chart which are divided up into twelve 30-degree segments to make up the complete horoscope of

360 degrees. As the planets move through the zodiac, they emphasize these different areas of your love life.

The Phases of the Moon

The cycle of the Moon lasts approximately 30 days as it appears to move round the zodiac. We usually notice the Full Moon because this is when the Sun is directly opposite the Moon and casts its light upon the Moon's surface. The Moon only stays in one sign for about two to three days and will influence your personal Sun sign for a few days every month. The other phases of the Moon which effect your Sun sign are the New Moon, the First Quarter Moon and the Last Quarter Moon. For example, a New Moon on June 29 in Cancer will be followed by a First Quarter Moon a week later, then a Full Moon about one week later, a Last Quarter Moon a week after that, and another New Moon on July 29 in Leo. The New Moon is a time to start out on a new quest, adventure or love affair. Make plans for the month ahead, make that phone call, go on a first date. The First Quarter Moon is for seduction and persuasion. The Full Moon is a critical turning point in the Moon's cycle when it's time to make decisions, face your true feelings or complete what you set out to do under the New Moon. The Last Quarter Moon is for being realistic about your relationship.

Lunar/Solar Eclipses

These happen a few times a year and used to be considered bad omens by the ancients. Actually, they just bring into focus personal issues you might be avoiding or are not aware need attention in your relationships. A Lunar eclipse is when the Earth gets in the way of the Sun's light shining on a Full Moon and there appears to be a dark shadow moving across the Moon. The easiest way to remember what a Lunar eclipse means is to say 'the present blots out the past'. (The Moon is usually associated with past in astrology.) For example, whatever issues you need to clarify in your current relationship, think about them; don't dwell on the past. A Solar eclipse is when the Moon gets in the way of the Sun, so we lose it's light temporarily at various places on Earth. The easiest way to interpret a Solar eclipse is to say 'the past blots out the future'. (The Sun is usually associated with the future.) For example, there are things which you have bottled up, denied or avoided from your past patterns of behaviour which now need attention before you can get on with the future of your current relationship.

The Elements

Each Sun sign is also one of the four elements. It's useful to know them because signs that are of the same element are often highly compatible.

The element of Fire: Aries, Leo, Sagittarius. The Fire signs are highly motivated, passionate visionaries.

The element of Earth: Taurus, Virgo, Capricorn. The Earth signs are sensualists who build solid relationships.

The element of Air: Gemini, Libra, Aquarius. The Air signs are romantic geniuses.

The element of Water: Cancer, Scorpio, Pisces. The Water signs are sultry, sexual lovers.

Your Love
Horoscope
2004

Aries

The Ram

March 21 – April 20

Love Check

Why you're fabulous

 There's no-one who can rival you when it comes to hunting or chasing the lover of your dreams.

 You're bold and dynamic and always the first to take the initiative.

Why you're impossible

 Sometimes you're impatient for sex and want it all NOW.

 Relationships with no challenges and no fun don't last long.

Your love secrets

 Romantic but feisty, you don't want the thrill of the chase to ever end.

 You're not easily led astray, except by your imagination.

 You don't want to be hunted yourself.

Your sexual style

Direct, passionate, volatile and competitive.

Who falls for you

Romantic idealists or dynamic career types who know you're as fiery and as motivated as they are.

Who you fall for

Someone who picks up the pieces when you've stormed around the place creating chaos. Earthy sensualists and dark horses.

You identify with

Celebrities, crusaders, heroes and heroines. Anyone who has a 'mission impossible' and succeeds.

Your greatest temptation

Falling in love with someone already involved.

Your greatest strength

Determination to win at any cost.

Passion Profile for 2004

Take the road towards a new challenging love and what you truly desire will follow. Hunt hard, passionately and with self-belief – you're going to be amazed by the choice ahead of you. Right from January you're getting the kind of reaction you love best – dynamic, absorbing and challenging. And all year you can be assured of endless romantic possibilities and scenarios. Make it a year to stand by your self-respect and don't let anyone topple you from your favourite love nest. There will be friends who squirm with envy as you prove you're irrepressible when it comes to seducing the love of your life midsummer. Your ruler Mars makes your greatest fantasies come true – and if you look after number one, you'll be sure to have the kind of year which can only be described as feeling like a 'sexual squillionaire'.

2004 Month by Month

January

With such a seductive ability to organize yourself and everyone else this month it's hardly surprising that you'll be flourishing in the limelight of friends and lovers. When you make an entrance around the 16th, do so with verve and a touch of panache. Cause a stir and you will be noticed.

Early on in the month, when confronted by close partners or lovers, you could feel that life has suddenly begun to aim its arrows straight on target for your heart. But your normal brilliant way of covering up the truth of your feelings will provide little hiding place. You have to open up – and you have to respond in kind. With Mars in your own fiery, passionate sign and Venus in your secret zone from the 15th, the feelings you have for romance and harmony will fuel you with enough energy for socializing and responding in the only way you know how. And that's with the passion and drive to show your lover that you truly care, even though you need to maintain your independence. The New Moon on the 21st intensifies your ability to try to communicate some of those rather powerful feelings, so speak out while he's in the mood to listen. With Saturn and Mercury backtracking through your chart, it would be wise to avoid any discussions about serious long-term commitments this month. Freedom is in your mind and keeping your head clear and focussed is probably a safer bet than rushing headlong into a promise that you might regret later.

February

The trouble with being a passionate and dramatic Fire sign is that you can often, quite unintentionally, inflict more hurt on those around you than you imagine. This month, with so much going on for you personally, you might even not notice the moods of a partner or lover, in your joy at being yourself. So take care after the 3rd, when your ruler Mars plunges on into Taurus, when you might just say something costly and then wish you hadn't been so impulsive. But luck is on your side too, as Venus moves into your own sign on the 9th to give you charisma, self-belief and a whole new sense of personal achievement. Around the 10th, communicate clearly what your intentions are concerning your relationship, because by the 20th you'll be frantically energetic for romantic treats and sexual and physical pleasure, and you'll be wanting more and more time to spend in each other's arms.

Try as you might, your partner just won't bend to your rules and you may be forced to make hasty rearrangements by the 26th. But with Mercury moving into Pisces on the 26th, he should at least begin to understand the drama behind your motives and you can release all that energetic generosity and enthusiasm into some sexy strategies aimed to please.

If you're single, the powerful planetary activity this month brings a run of mood swings. One day you think, 'What's the point of relationships anyway?', the next you're gazing at beautiful men in the street and flirting with your best friend's boyfriend. It's time to admit that past affairs may not have worked out as you hoped, but deep down you want to have some romantic fun. Around the 17th, phone that male colleague who's been dying to take you out. In fact, if there's no adventure in your life you'll seize up like a clam, so go out and create new romantic events rather than assume they're going to appear on a silver platter. You need to hunt and chase, not to sit on the sidelines without a challenge.

March

Living your life as if it were a game of chance or just one long adventure is certainly one way of fulfilling your potential. But refusing to see the truth because it might just not be as magical as you would like it to be can cause you to make or break relationships too easily. An intimate friendship could seem in jeopardy around the first two weeks of March, as Mercury cruises into your own sign on the 12th, and you're simply not willing to listen to their excuses about why they've been avoiding you. Don't take it personally, they simply fear you haven't got any time for them, so make it clear that you have now. With the Sun and a New Moon enhancing your own sign on the 20th, you redeem yourself and realize that sometimes you have to accept reality. Now you'll begin to sparkle and any social events or dos could be great places to meet potential new partners. Just don't give up on an existing one because you're feeling a little rampant. Yes, you must decide if you want to continue in this challenging way, but it only takes a little self-awareness to realize that if you're not on the hunt for something then you're instantly bored.

Conquests pile up if you're single, and if you're attached, just take care with your lover's heart after the 15th, when that green-eyed monster could be facing you across a dinner table and, of course, innocent as you are, you cause a silly, but highly-frantic misunderstanding. By the end of March, the twinkle in your eye has returned and your sense of humour is gaining you the kind of attention and love that you truly deserve.

April

Impulse and reason rarely walk hand in hand for you and this month, with your ruler Mars squaring up to Jupiter around the 4th, watch out that sparks don't fly. You might feel you're missing something in one relationship and then propel yourself very quickly into another without thinking of the consequences. But even early on in the month you have a restless need to cut ties and look for new blood. As much as you appear to be independent or carefree about love, loneliness is not something you care for.

With passions running high around the 14th, jealousy and possessiveness could be dangerous territory if you're single. 'Mistrustful, me? Never' you insist, but you may well find you have a few irrational and very irritating suspicions all the same. Particularly when you find yourself infatuated with a male colleague who's already involved. His merest glance at someone else could spark off criticism or moodiness in you. Then you imagine he's sending text messages to everyone in the office, except you. It's fine to be an observer or life, but not if you turn every fleeting moment of insecurity into a major drama. By the 18th, you come back down to earth again when you bump into him in the corridor and realize he's soul-less.

Don't let an important meeting pass you by on the 19th, when the New Moon in your own sign heralds a new romantic liaison or change of heart. And don't get muddled up by making too many promises too quickly.

May

The month is filled with a few tense moments and extremes of energy, particularly around the Full Moon on the 4th in Scorpio. With Jupiter's forward motion on the 5th, you're suddenly the bees knees when it comes to partying, socializing and flirting at all kinds of work outings. Make the most of being the centre of attention and smile charmingly at one admirer. They could be useful to you later in the year.

With your ruler Mars surging on into Cancer from the 7th, you wonder if anyone is ever going to understand your emotional needs and maybe it's just time you owned up and admitted you have feelings as much as anyone else. But one partner or lover begins to wonder if you've lost that old passion and zest for life. Prove them wrong on the 17th, even though Venus turns retrograde in Gemini. It is people out there who are subdued – they're the ones putting off dates and generally feeling tested by love's little mysteries. You, on the other hand, are passion-filled and raring to go. Love seems to be taking up so much of your time this month you're wondering when you'll be free to be you again. And anticipating a challenging romantic situation is wise as the month draws to a close. It might just be the tonic you need to remind yourself that when it comes to relationships you need to take a few risks and gambles along the way or you wouldn't be you.

June

With Venus tracking backwards in your friendship zone until the 29th, you still worry why certain lovers or partners are keeping a low profile. But the Full Moon in Sagittarius on the 3rd has bathed your whole love life in a tantalizing light. You are the sole creator of plots and intrigue in your sexual affairs, and your erotic aura attracts an equally charismatic reaction from your lover. On the 12th, you feel that love has taken a different route from the path you had planned. Crossroads are challenges, not restrictions, and they add impetus to your dynamic approach to someone special. But working too hard at love takes the pleasure of romance away – and plans that may have been carefully crafted will have to be rethought by the 20th.

Your energy-saving grace comes after the 24th, when your ruler Mars sweeps on into fiery Leo. Love may burn, enflame or ignite all over the place, so take care if you're already involved with some-one. Any commitment you have already made to a relationship seems heavier and more of a burden than your normal wild and adventurous nature can handle. But it will give you a sense of the wider implications that a harmonious partnership can bring. As the month comes to an end, all the signs are that the love you have so far been given is nowhere near as great as the love you could make in the following months.

If you're single, watch out for fireworks on the 18th, when Uranus brings you an unexpected but fascinating encounter. He might not be the man of your dreams, but he's fun and exciting, so enjoy some sexual adventure and romantic spontaneity while it's yours to play with. More than anything else, don't feel you have to live by other people's expectations. You're proving you have vision, self-belief and practical common sense, but, most of all, you are an individual in your own right, a star among other stars, but one that is truly shining the brightest on the world stage.

July

Though you're not fond of overt emotional scenes, you are beginning to understand how to handle a sensitive relationship. Without your energy and your drive being depleted, you realize that someone has a will of their own too. And now, with the powerful aspect between the Sun and Saturn on the 8th, you begin to accept that your rush to win love may be a rashness you have to learn to respect rather than try to destroy.

With Mars opposing Neptune on the 16th, seduction plays a big part in proving you're in control of one relationship. But you also begin to mistrust having too much sexual dependency on one person and feel it's time to untie a few knots and head for the open road. The Full Moon on the 2nd makes you want to aim for the top of your professional tree and forget about committed relationships, but the New Moon on the 17th makes you crave for some kind of stability. But while those ambivalent feelings last, you turn to your social life and begin to accept that you can't have it both ways. By the end of the month, your sexual and emotional needs seem more in tandem and the motivation to take a more responsible attitude towards your relationship grows. Venus's powerful tension with Pluto on the 24th triggers off a feeling that not all romantic attractions lead to something wonderful. In fact, you begin to turn down offers instead of turning up the heat every time you bump into a beautiful face.

With work commitments a high priority and family still making demands on your time, you yearn for summer romance. Take advantage of your ruler Mars's fiery energy and go on an adventure. If alone, at least you'll have time to discover if you're on the right track where one love interest is concerned.

August

Caution is not a word that you use very often in your vocabulary. But with the planetary activity this month you might find yourself caught in scenarios you'd rather avoid. Then you start thinking maybe, just maybe, I ought to take a more careful approach about getting involved with people who just aren't worth the effort. With Mars streaking on into Virgo on the 10th and Mercury back-tracking through your chart, it pays to work out whose side you're actually on. There will be smart, polished, well-dressed admirers around, there will be slick know-it-alls and cool customers, but discrimination is all. In fact, one or two suave sophisticates could turn out to be arrogant bores beneath the designer suits and the chic perfume.

By the middle of the month, your usual high spirits are fired up by new love and rekindled lust. Not only are close friends and social events playing an important role in your life now, but they're also beginning to make you see that the person you care most about needs a gentler approach. Hot-headed though you are, sometimes the dreamers of life hold you fascinated, and one such person either already in your life or a sudden fascination in the summertime heat makes you realize you can sometimes be a player as well as a leader.

With Venus in a sensitive area of your chart from the 7th onwards, you might have to face resentment or bittersweet moments from someone who thinks you can be too vain at times, and also too impulsive and demanding. Don't take it personally. They're just envious of your flamboyant behaviour and dynamic attitude to life and love. The feelings will pass and you'll begin to make decisions about where you are going in life and whether you want to be there alone or as a double act.

September

Relax and enjoy the thrills and spills of your life unfold in a provocative and exciting way this month. The first half of the month is for planning, for dedicating yourself to looking good and for indulging in your favourite sport – romance. As you move into the second week of September, you begin to get restless for fun and for sexier, more scintillating company. It's not that you don't care about one special person but just maybe they're not enough or don't fulfil those things you really need in life. Which are, of course, a partner who can get up at the crack of dawn and drive off into the sunrise on a whim, or someone who will be a friend, lover and partner in any adventure.

By the third week of September, you're beginning to see how romance and pleasure are fundamental to your happiness and existence. The Sun moves into Libra after the 22nd and, lo and behold, the last week of the month looks set to be the most creative, both romantically and sexually. With Jupiter firing on into Libra on the 25th and Mars following in its wake on the 26th, you suddenly find it's raining relationships. There just seems to be so much choice, you don't know whether you're coming or going, or who's doing what to whom. You go on dates which on the surface seem to offer excitement, but they just don't bring you the magic you're looking for. Then suddenly, your social life rises a few octaves and a few heads turn. This time they're the kind you love the best. Now the hunt is on and you've got some pretty luscious and seductive prey out there, particularly around the 27th after Mars and Jupiter's dynamic collusion, and you just can't stop smiling. So don't resist those temptations, party till you drop and fall head over heels in love with every face you dance with.

This is your month for stunning relationships, sexy text messages, enchanting phone calls, wicked whispers and sexual pleasure. Platonic relationships with the opposite sex are really the last thing on your mind, physical passion is the first. So just take care you don't double date or double up too often without seriously considering the consequences. Hearts could get hurt – and that means yours too. But there is one person out there who could become a long-term dream. Remember to look before you leap though – you don't want laundry and slippers in front of the log fire, you want the kind of heat that keeps you chasing each other forever.

October

Well, you have to calm down sometimes, just to raise the temperature and hot up the pace again later. But with those two roguish planets Mars and Jupiter still lifting your spirits, bringing hustlers, larger-than-life *amours* and social encounters of the most magical kind into your life, you really are spoilt for choice.

Watch out for the two eclipses this month which will test your courage and honesty. There's a partial Solar eclipse on the 14th in Libra and with Mercury moving on into Scorpio on the 15th you might feel as if you have to give an all-or-nothing answer to a very personal question. But do you want to? Can't you just avoid the subject and not have to commit yourself to opening your mouth? By the Lunar eclipse on the 28th, you'll realize what it is you have to relinquish from your past. No tears, no regrets; just admit that you were wrong and remind yourself that the future is far more important than old mistakes. Nostalgic, you? Hardly, but there are moments when you wish the earth would open up and swallow you. But with a growing sense of self-belief, you move on with a wry smile and a feeling that if you hadn't opened up and revealed the truth, you wouldn't have fresh hopes and dreams of a magical kind of love.

With Venus moving into Libra on the 29th, enriching warmth for someone develops and you begin to act and love in the way that suits you best – with energy, inspiration and endless vision for the future.

November

That very romantic association you recently made will intensify and deepen, and perhaps lead to a full-blown sexual affair by the New Moon of the 12th.

With Mars moving into Scorpio on the 11th and Venus following on the 22nd, you're beginning to find that the intricacies of sexual relating are far more complex than you thought. Dark, mysterious strangers could come into your life, or one light-hearted, fun-loving friendship becomes more torrid and fraught with emotional implications. You begin to realize that fulfilling your own sexual needs is more important to you than any social whirl or professional coup. And it's a time when you could make or break friendships if they don't fit in with your lifestyle. But by the 25th you must try to communicate your needs to someone special. With Uranus beginning to push forward in your chart again on the 11th, you can at least begin to see more clearly where your ideals about love and relationships are leading you. If you truly want a better, closer, more free yet passionate double act, then this is the month when with clarity and honesty you can make it clear what you really want from that lover. Whether in bed or out of it, the rules of the game will change. Every relationship has its own dynamic, so be prepared to be challenged and liberated and to learn a lot. Your sexual moods will be invigorated and intensified, and if you're already in a long-lasting, binding love affair, then this month you might feel that you're as restless in love as you are in spirit.

December

You can begin to relax more, play more and learn from your self-sufficient nature. Taking risks is one of your greatest pleasures in life, whether it's anything from driving fast to doing the most outrageous things associated with fast-paced living. With both Venus and Mars surging on into Sagittarius this month, you're hellbent on having your way and just getting on with every romantic adventure possible.

The month starts with outdoor fun – and your mood lightens by the New Moon on the 12th when you're generally more optimistic about life with your lover or partner. If you're still single and want to keep it that way, then social fun and pre-Christmas games will sparkle with attractions and flirtations. Whether single or attached, the lighter and the more emotionally distanced you can maintain any relationship now, the easier you will feel. The pure childlike innocence of your romantic desires can overcome even the most difficult seduction act and by the end of the month you can relax and know that there is someone out there who wants you as much as you want them. The critical time for a head-on clash of words or acceptance of each other's desire will be around the 21st. But remember, your personal love life is always tinged with chance taking or the love of dangerous liaisons.

This month, the emotion and intensity of your feelings are what leads you on to a whole new wave of creative relating and sexual fulfilment. It's time to say you can't be anyone else than yourself, and if someone special can understand and accept your personal need for independence and good living, then festive happiness is yours and love waits under every twig of mistletoe.

Your Love
Horoscope
2004

Taurus
The Bull

April 21 – May 20

Your Love
Horoscope
2004

Love Check

Why you're fabulous

 Serene and sensual, you live for every moment of love without worrying about the past.

 You adore the seduction game – the longer it goes on the better.

 Earthy and smoochy, you have a stabilizing effect on your partner.

Why you're impossible

 When you see someone beautiful to the eye you just have to own them.

 Your attitude to finances can cause more ups and downs in your relationships than anything else.

Your love secrets

 A connoisseur of the good things in life, your hedonist desires are often underrated.

 You often accuse your partner of being the jealous possessive one when it's really you.

Passive seduction is your innate art, you don't have to cultivate it.

Your sexual style

Feral, primeval and slowly arousing.

Who falls for you

Sexually-dominating powerful partners who want to possess you. Earthy pragmatists who realize you're as shrewd in the bedroom as out of it.

Who you fall for

Hypnotic, intense partners who are also sensually beautiful and very mysterious, or fiery visionaries who don't know how to sit down and relax.

You identify with

Financial wizardry, beauty and nature. Connoisseurs of the luxuries and pleasures of life.

Your greatest temptation

Men who are impossibly vain and refuse to catch your eye.

Your greatest strength

The patience to wait for him to realize you're worth every moment of your time spent doing so.

Passion Profile for 2004

This must be the one year that really brings you a change of heart regarding one relationship. It's not that you don't want commitment, you usually do – it makes you feel secure and content. And although someone hasn't exactly been falling at your feet, you're beginning to be convinced that you mean more to them than just a passing dream. With Mars cruising through your sign in February, it's time to test their passion for you. Is it real, or is it just a game? Either way, don't turn it into a fanatical arm-wrestle. Not that you're about to leap off into the sunset chasing them around town either. But by mid-summer you are feeling driven to be a catalyst and you are ready to be a missile for love if you have to be.

This is a year when intense experiences, moving moments, albeit laced with a fear that you might be rejected, have to be confronted. But do you want simplicity, sofas, candlelight and cosy *tête-à-têtes*, or a liaison sprinkled with uncertainty? Don't make any decisions until late November – you owe it to yourself to go softly softly. Enjoy every romantic moment for what it is and don't place those great expectations on the big 'it' too quickly, or too soon. Instead, spoon-feed your personal needs and draw a long, sensuous bath.

2004 Month by Month

January

The year begins with Saturn forcing you to focus on new relationship goals and encouraging you to make a few New Year's resolutions to declutter your mind and emotions. Aspirations become serious as Venus allows you a glimpse of what you truly want, but indecision will keep you from grabbing it until the 6th, when Mercury starts to move forward in your chart. By the 15th, you're beginning to throw all sexual inhibitions aside and you can develop and open up the expressive side of yourself. Through this kind of honesty, you can work out who and what matters to you most.

Ideals, ambition and material progress top your agenda all month and you're determined to prove that you're capable of doing more than your best where one intimate partner is concerned. As Venus aligns with Uranus on the 14th, you become a little rebellious and you're thinking of nothing but your personal needs. Selfish acts can be highly sexually charged and, as long as it's legal, you're free to indulge yourself and others in all your mutual desires and fantasies. After the 20th, you're blessed with a charismatic aura, so charm a well-heeled admirer from the corridors of power. Use enchanting words to seduce this designer-suited lover into eminently satisfying your libido. But no-one can tie you down this month, now you're determined to follow your own path.

Around the New Moon of the 21st, a new and harmonious friendship highlights your sensitivity and you hanker for life's refined, ephemeral pleasures. Labels and flashy cars are not enough, you want someone who shares your love of beauty. Watch out for a pleasant surprise after the Sun has moved into Aquarius on the 22nd – it could be you bump into a lover you've been trying to forget. He's dead gorgeous, pretty ephemeral and he's got a vivid recollection of all your favourite fantasies. Reminisce together.

February

Dreamy days thinking about that rediscovered secret *amour* remind you how important love and romance are, and, hard as you try, you can't shut them out. Around the 1st, joining a club or returning to circles you once moved in helps re-establish magical bonds and news of long-lost friends brings a heavenly nostalgic air. After the 3rd, Mars surges into your own sign to give you bags of energy and a determination to be passionate about life and love.

The Full Moon on the 6th gives the impression that your romantic and professional dreams are coming true. But consider carefully what it is you really want or you might just receive the attention of one rogue who proves to be more than a little complex. Around the 13th, a moment's unreliability from this friendly flirt gives a hint of things to come. He might seem like a good catch, but he just won't be caught.

When the Sun moves into Pisces on the 19th, you'll find the confidence to discuss your personal needs with a new flame. Suggest you go public to test the depth of their commitment to discover just how serious they are. Unless he can give you what you need, cut the cord. Around the 24th, you'll have a string of dazzling suitors fighting to indulge your every whim. Stop giving too much too soon and learn to receive – it's a sure-fire way to sensual bliss.

March

Thanks to Venus moving into your sign on the 6th, you're seductively sizzling and radiating charisma, so relish the attention you attract this month.

If you're single, a kiss on the cheek from a work colleague could turn into something more serious by the 20th. While Mercury's in your mystery zone after the 12th, hold your cards close to your chest – you don't want to give the game away to your friends about how you feel about him, not yet anyway. From the 11th, your attention is distracted by work or by another very cool customer, and you'll be juggling sexual desires with professional obligations. Business is best avoided on the 17th, when your craving for the easy life gets you tangled up in too many love interests, lowering your ability to concentrate on work.

If you're attached, personal celebrations with a lover boost your libido around the 10th. Then around the 21st Mars moves out of your own sign and heightens your need to create a closer, more sensual bond. But grounding your romantic ideals isn't quite as easy as you thought. And with Pluto's reversal in your chart on the 24th, you begin to wonder if he really feels the same way as you do. A real heart-to-heart on the 27th gives you a chance to work things out and you realize there's more than just a momentary glimpse of potential happiness in his eyes. He finds you generous, gorgeous and downright perfect.

April

Mercury's backward motion in your own sign between the 5th and the 30th makes you pernickety and partners or lovers get the sharp end of your tongue. Especially if they suggest anything which hasn't been thought out. Play devil's advocate at work on the 10th and your brilliant debating skills will outwit the opposition and impress a very sexy colleague to boot. Give the benefit of your experience in a one-to-one meeting and decide if it's worth taking a chance for a flirtatious night out. Are they interested in you, or is it a ploy to get their hands on insider information? By the 15th, you're on a libido high and your sensual desire takes over decision making. Throw caution to the wind, give the filing to the temp, and enjoy a weekend of complete abandon.

On the 14th, Venus's wrangle with Jupiter upsets your plans for a gourmet night in with a special person. It's not that they aren't tempted by what you have to offer, just that they're playing a game of their own. And by the 20th, when the Sun enters your own sign, the balance of one relationship enters a whole new phase. This time round make sure it's your mind as well as your physical needs that's in control, because this is one month when hearts could get broken if there is nothing real and tangible between you. It's not that you want this relationship to end, but if it can't stand the test of true love, then what is it to you anyway? Stop trying to take control of your partner's every move and you won't be let down by love's mysterious ways ever.

May

Party frolics abound all month and you're so popular you don't know which to attend. With your ruler Venus dominating your financial arena, it's tough to separate work from pleasure, so head for those which offer excellent networking opportunities. The way you mingle and wax lyrical is devastatingly attractive and you're soon surrounded by a circle of sexy, influential admirers.

Around the Full Moon in Scorpio on the 4th, free yourself up to enjoy life's more physical pleasures. Forget the mind – yes, you've done all that brainstorming last month – and instead indulge in a wicked physical liaison with someone you least expected. Don't harbour any hopes beyond scorching sex and you won't be disappointed. While emotional attachments can be draining, physical pleasures will fortify you this month. After the 16th, old flames make a reappearance and new ones arrive on the scene. So stand back and take a very objective look at what your real needs are. You'll see more clearly by distancing yourself romantically from the past. And you'll realize how important it is to be open-minded and that the devil you know isn't always the best option.

Take a week off from emotional demands on the 20th, and when you flick through the latest sensational events in your diary it brings them all back to life. And once again you can realize how satisfying your sensual needs is your passport to happiness.

Sailing through your own or friends' birthday celebrations, you're a calming influence on everyone you meet, including any partner that you've recently found impossible to live with. Suddenly they're bedazzled, and so are you, and you'll be so adored on the 25th that you'll reach higher emotional levels than you've ever experienced before. And do you know how sizzlingly attractive that is?

June

With so much planetary energy focussed on your relationships this month, it's hardly surprising you're in the mood for sensual pleasure, so delight your lover or boyfriend and spend some lovely moments together around the time of the Full Moon on the 3rd. If you're deeply involved in a relationship then you'll feel ready to indulge in the kind of pleasure that only Taureans can imagine. Blissful and erotic, languid and ravishing. You'll be in such an earthy mood you'll send shivers of desire down your lover's spine, so enjoy a mutual massage and share an indulgent bedtime feast.

The theme for this month is to be prepared for intimate secrets to be shared around the 15th, when Mercury and the Sun give you the confidence to reveal your wildest dreams. What was it he said to you a few weeks ago, something deeply important that didn't seem so at the time? Think back to the past few weeks and you'll be pleasantly surprised by one of his chance remarks, especially when he says it again after the 20th.

If you're single, a dreamy male colleague turns out to be fascinated by your sensual aura. Now usually you don't do the chasing – the very art of Taurean seductive skills is to be alluring but passive. Actually, in this case, it could be worth making a suggestive comment or showing your interest – flirting, teasing or perhaps coincidentally leaving the building at the same time. Don't worry about coming on too strong. Your nature demands you be simmering rather than boiling with desire, and you're hardly likely to rush down the steps after him in film-star fashion demanding you go out to lunch. Better to remain your sophisticated self, to be quietly and shrewdly alert to his notice of you, and then keep him drooling until after the 25th, by which time your languorous seduction will pay off.

July

Unnecessary but unavoidable ties have weighed you down over the past few months, but as the summer sun bathes you in a radiant glow, they will begin to feel lighter. Feelings of frustration because you still can't escape certain responsibilities could force you into saying things you don't really mean to someone close. Wait until the end of the month and you'll be true to yourself when you finally speak up. Whatever you've been feeling haunted by recently you'll now be able to tackle with renewed vigour and a sense of 'it's got to come out in the wash, so I'll make sure it's squeaky clean when it does'.

There's a considerable amount of intrigue going on in your social circle and although you're usually known for your tact, you could impetuously tell someone a story without thinking of the consequences around the 13th. Whatever happens, make sure you really think about what you want to express and what you truly need to tell a close friend. After all, your spontaneous mood won't last for long and you'll probably find yourself patiently listening to the advice of others instead. Play it cool for a while – after the 19th, you'll know that you were right to take a moment's caution.

On the 26th, you'll want to break new ground in your social circle. It's almost as if someone radically different is making you aware that it's time to get cracking and make exciting plans for the future. Even if it's simply a party or fun-packed day of adventure, go out and be your most dynamic and active self.

August

Seize the chance to prove to a boyfriend or new *amour* you're ready for deeper intimacy and emotional bliss. Expand his awareness of what your sexual needs are and show him how easy it is to give and take pleasure in true Taurean sensual style.

On the 18th, you could suddenly feel less enthusiastic about how deeply he actually feels for you, and if you're convinced he's keeping a subtle distance for a few days, then take a breathing space yourself. You know you can be incredibly possessive when you're feeling vulnerable, so go out and enjoy yourself with your closest pal, get a new perspective on your life, or keep yourself occupied so that those feelings don't drown you in anxiety or worry. Excessive thinking means you need to channel those thoughts and those deeper sexual desires into something solid and pleasurable. So indulge yourself in your favourite food just for one day and be provocative and flirtatious with a stranger in the bar or coffee shop. Strong feelings like this don't last but projecting them on your boyfriend or man will only make him feel claustrophobic. Don't worry, by the New Moon in Leo on the 16th, you'll be amazed at his reaction to you. The biggest hugs and kisses you could ever imagine. Who could have thought you could be so crazy to think he doesn't care?

September

Around the 4th, a sudden spark of inspiration about changing your future aims could make for some nail-biting moments. Dealing with other people's changing scenarios and ability to make sudden and often impulsive gestures isn't easy for you, and when it comes to your own future and lifestyle, you need to make changes slowly and carefully. To ensure your long-term happiness is assured, you need to do some rational thinking. Don't get persuaded by someone to make the wrong decision. Think about what kind of relationship makes you feel good to be you and then make it clear to your lover what you really want. Take the initiative, speak up, send it in a letter if you have to. But don't forget to listen to your most profound and inner of voices. Whatever the external event that triggers your need to sort out your feelings, with growing awareness you'll actually know what is right and what is wrong for you. By the 25th, with Jupiter moving into Libra, you'll be inclined to celebrate your breakthrough instead of pooh-poohing it, so go pop a few corks.

The end of September is all about playing, and with Mars and Jupiter triggering off a feeling that more than anything you need harmony in your love life, you could find yourself totally committed to a sensual and deeply moving experience with your lover. If you're single, watch out, this could be the magical chemistry that moves you into a powerfully magnetic attraction. So enjoy yourself. This month is about letting go of painful memories and beginning slowly to unwind from the pressures of the past few months.

October

There's a Lunar eclipse in your own sign on the 28th, so make this a month to really enjoy feeling in tune and in harmony with your friends, lovers and even work colleagues.

With Venus in Virgo from the 3rd, the whole month is bathed in a settled and warm-hearted glow for you. Your social life will be coloured with loving and affectionate feelings, and because you are so deeply aware of your moods, you also know that when you seem at your most laid-back on the surface, you're deeply determined to succeed underneath. The undercurrents of powerful Taurean energy are now bubbling slowly and quietly. That's because Mercury enters your relationship zone on the 15th and your intuition is telling you – find out about October. It feels like it's going to be great and there's a sense of romantic anticipation in the air. And from the 10th, if you're attached, the celestial activity vitalizes the interactive side of your relationship. So it's time for you to communicate your feelings to your lover. Quite honestly, the sexier the message the better. This is a time when you are able to truly tell him how you feel and, more crucially, what you expect from this relationship. It's now or never to get it right, so make it clear you have to honour your own needs as well as his.

November

Sexually, you're absolutely consumed with lust around the New Moon on the 12th. And you really can't miss out on that close bond you've begun to develop between you and one special person. This month, take advantage of your wonderful aura and let your lover see the quality of earthy sensuality that you possess. It will do wonders for your social life as well, so go out and enjoy frivolous fun and show off your warm charisma.

If you're single, watch out for a delicious attraction down those corridors of power after the 11th, when Mars surges on into sexy Scorpio. Someone's spotted you, but have you noticed them yet? Your keen senses will tell you when you meet up. Whether it's body language or a chemical reaction, your sexual hunting can now be put to the test. Don't wait too long – trust in your intuition and gut reaction.

Rustle those silk sheets with your lover on the Full Moon night of the 26th and exchange sexual fantasies – the moment is right for unadulterated pleasure. If you're single, dress to kill or to hunt, and seduce a new man at a social whirl. Mind you, there's a few friends who need your loyalty around the 23rd, so however much you're feeling frisky, remember that your practical advice will keep someone else sane.

December

Around the 2nd, you have feelings of temporary confusion about your relationships and close friends. But don't worry, although you're now ready to speak openly about how you feel, the response you desire will be utterly magical. What you do need to take care of is other people's demands and assumptions this month. Are you being pushed into making compromises, or do you truly want to go your own way this Christmas? The truth will out by the 15th, when you finally realize that what you truly value and what you truly need in life is more important than what others expect from you.

After the New Moon on the 12th, one loved one needs some reassurance – be your most caring and tender self and you'll be rewarded with a passionate response. Sexually, you could feel liberated by new insight into someone's feelings or needs and responses. You'll also feel an unusual need to express yourself around the Full Moon of the 26th, so enjoy and indulge in some long and blissful moments with your lover. Whatever they say to you now they truly mean, as long as they aren't up to their ears in a melange of Christmas spirits. Seriously, you know that more than anything you need constancy and devotion in your life, not necessarily extremes of behaviour to prove it, but enough to demonstrate that you are loved for who you are not what others think you may be. Make the end of the year one when your physical needs and your emotional make-up are honestly clarified and respected.

Your Love
Horoscope
2004

Gemini

The Twins

May 21 – June 20

Love Check

Why you're fabulous

- You always put a smile on other people's faces.
- Men find your witty, light-hearted approach to life magical.
- Pals love hearing you gossip on the phone.

Why you're impossible

- You can't keep a secret.
- Making up your mind where to eat out drives him crazy.

Your love secrets

- You flirt with your best friend's man.
- All that superficial fun disguises a very sensitive soul.
- When you're trying to catch a man you never let on you are.

Your sexual style

- Unpredictable, cheeky, but utterly romantic.

Who falls for you

Down-to-earth rugged hunks who admire your brain or want to control your scattered approach to life. Light-hearted gamblers who just want to have fun.

Who you fall for

Independent freedom-lovers, travellers and gurus, or men who can tell you stories in bed all night. Or you go to the other extreme and hook into dreamy, elusive types.

You identify with

Communicators, mobile phone fanatics and anyone who's up for the latest gossip.

Your greatest temptation

Having two boyfriends in case one rejects you.

Your greatest strength

You'd rather know the truth than live in a fantasy world.

Passion Profile for 2004

Searching for a deeper truth, you cleverly allow your heart to rule your head more than ever this year. The first few months of the year you're in a light-hearted mood, discussing dreams and ideals within a sizzling relationship. With the passionate influence of Mars in your sign from March 21, you're charismatic and impulsive enough to reinvent yourself to please a serious lover, or just enjoy the fact you're single and loving all the attention. Pluto's move forward at the end of August awakens your need for relationship change and it evolves into a highly personal, internal transformation. You may have to give up a very special part of yourself, be it your heart, your virginity or your independence. But change opens up exciting new doors and in the autumn you're making serious love commitments. By December, you'll have found a balance between the physical and emotional aspects of your relationships and they're travelling side by side. You develop your right to independence, while still maintaining deep feelings for a partner all year. It's hard to improve on that, so soar into 2004 with your head in those clouds. For once, your romantic dreams are real and you can turn them into reality.

2004 Month by Month

January

Getting decked out to boost your professional image, you attract gorgeously unexpected attention which has nothing to do with work. Handsome hunks smoulder at bus stops and coffee counters, thanks to your new image and confident aura early January. If you're aiming for a promotion or raise, you'll see a positive response if you use subtlety to flirt your way to your desires, while Saturn's backtracking through Cancer.

Make use of Mercury's change of direction from the 6th onwards to think clearly about your unpredictable streak when it comes to one confusing liaison. You know you've been trying to seduce this rogue for some time, but you're also astute enough to realize he may just be one big tease. Around the 14th, you encounter him socially and flirt and play the romantic game, but he just doesn't seem to respond in the way you'd truly like. Find solace in the words of a male friend or colleague instead. With the influence of racy Mars on the 23rd, you could find solace in his bed too.

With energy levels peaking, thanks to Venus moving into Pisces on the 15th, you can experience a marathon of arousal and discover pleasure in unusual places. Spice up the workplace by staying late and making love when everyone's gone home, but check out where the cameras are hidden first. Work takes on a whole new thrilling dimension and gives you a heady few days around the 27th, when you'll be bending over backwards to accommodate certain colleagues, in more ways than one.

February

Launch yourself onto the social circuit from the 1st and put your energy into helping friends with preparations for a fun Valentine's bash. Organizing a fabulously alternative party is just what you need to take your mind off a relationship problem. Mars's move into Taurus on the 3rd makes you wonder if you're still in that special lover's good books. Luckily, the Full Moon on the 6th provides friends and gatherings to take your mind onto higher planes. Mercury's move through Aquarius throughout February makes you question whether an idealistic dream of perfect love is really worth pursuing. It is, but first you need to change. Adopt a critical attitude towards your excessively high ideals or no partner can ever live up to them.

On the 15th, you're feeling ultra-sensitive and tempted to launch yourself headfirst into a wine bottle. With Valentine's day behind you, you begin to feel a little disillusioned about love, but the only real escape is to reach an understanding with your partner about what your mutual needs really are.

Mercury's collusion with Uranus on the 27th brings initiative and objectivity to help you handle your most confused of feelings. So use it to throw yourself into finding out what really arouses your partner and how you can bring more mutual acceptance into your relationship. Slowly your secret dreams are starting to be realized. Share your fantasies and by the 28th you'll be wallowing in popularity and back in the arms of someone special. Restrain your tendency to be over-impulsive all month and enjoy the magical prospect of the romantic entertainment that's there waiting you.

March

Dazzle friends, lovers and strangers by blazing an enthusiastic trail through their lives from the 12th, when Mercury lurches on into Aries bringing you a sparkling wit and charm. With itchy feet and a taste for frivolous romance, you want to meet mind-expanding rogues or just set off to exotic shores. So, around the Full Moon on the 6th, either organize a fun holiday or join a very male-oriented club. New blood is out there waiting for you, whatever your choice. But watch out, it's easy to get derailed and you could find yourself doing the walk of shame once too often this month.

Sexy opportunities come at you from every angle this month, but around the 17th even being outrageous becomes predictable and you're encouraged to do a little soul-searching. On the 18th, you see beyond the 'what is' towards the 'what if' and Mercury gives you dazzlingly unique ideas for an exciting new vision. Develop a plan and by the 24th, as the Sun moves into your chart's idealistic zone, you'll surge towards relationship success.

Beautiful sensual encounters become interesting again on the 28th, thanks to a delightful Venus. Then someone surprises you with a novel suggestion and the temperature rises. By the 31st, Mars provokes a directness to reveal exactly what you want, but to see what it is you have to look quite deeply within yourself and that's to prove you're not as innocent as you make out. Of course you could surprise yourself, but you're more likely to shock that gorgeous lover with your uninhibited sexual response. Get out the sex toys and let the games begin.

April

This is one of the months when your natural talent to fascinate others, not forgetting your wit and charm, can be put to wonderful advantage. Seductive Venus highlights your charismatic allure after the 4th, making you at your most persuasive and luckiest. Whenever you are out there in company, whether with friends or colleagues, you'll radiate your sophisticated spirit. Now is the time to articulate your greatest thoughts and ideas. You're brimming with confidence and that charming way you have with words begins to take effect. A rank outsider suddenly seems besotted with you. Make sure you remain enigmatic and elusive; he needs to hunt, not to be chased.

Change does wonders for the Gemini feelings and mind, and you need variety in love, so with your ruler Mercury doing a U-turn from the 5th to the 30th, you could suffer from feelings of boredom. Then you could start to feel defensive and uncertain about your own and everyone else's motives and reactions. But don't worry, the mood will pass, and by the 26th your ability to be mentally agile and emotionally in tune will return. Enjoy weedling out gossip, using your humour and quick wits to analyze and dissect a few love rivals who may have ulterior motives for their future plans. You'll be the first to untangle the information, so use your ingenuity to make your own mark where it counts.

Be gregarious and charming at a work meeting around the 14th and a sexy associate's mistake gives you an opportunity to pitch your best ideas. An unexpected, light-hearted conversation a few days later in the office kitchen or corridor turns out to be something more enriching and your promotion prospects are suddenly looking great.

May

If your current lover sees you've arrived at your chosen rendezvous before them, don't assume they'll think you're over-keen and do believe that sometimes your changing ephemeral nature is actually a bonus. Who really wants you to be always exactly the same every time you meet? What he loves about you is your unpredictability and your light-hearted flirtation with life itself. So don't worry, any misunderstandings and travel delays will be resolved by the end of the month.

Talking of travelling, a sudden urge to travel on the 6th reminds you how restless you've been. Take the opportunity to plan a vacation for next month while you're in the mood. Whatever the difficulties in getting out and about this month, take the opportunity to discover another side of yourself. Get sporty and join the gym, or advance your studies and join an evening class, and you could even meet the man of your dreams if you're single, or just fall for a stranger if you're attached.

If you're attached, however hard the communication barriers are this month, you're now ready to make major relationship changes. There's been so much pressure on you recently to make the break, either for better or worse. And with Venus's stalling effects in your own sign from May 17 right through to June 29, it's time to really sort things out. Whichever decision you make will be the right one. If you really can't face having to close one chapter of your life and open another, talk it through with a friend who understands on the 29th – you'll feel better for the objective input. So take a deep breath, confirm your feelings to yourself and your long-term happiness will be guaranteed.

June

Why is it other people always think you are nervous, twitchy and restless? Is it because they don't know actually how difficult it is to be both a genius of communication and yet have such deeply profound feelings about life and love? In fact, this month you'll be in the mood to restore your energy levels. You've had too much work and not enough play for the past few weeks, and you need space for romantic play or instant boredom strikes.

Even though Venus is still reversing through your own sign until the 29th, get yourself ready for a sexier mood, because this is a month when you need to take time out from the rat race. Okay, so you hate sitting around getting bored or tapping your fingers, so plan a sexy jaunt in the countryside or a cheap weekend break around the Gemini New Moon on the 17th. Then later on in the month, on the 30th, make sure you lubricate your limbs – go jogging or work out with your man. All this leisure stuff is essential while Venus is slowing your mental levels down and your usual energy peaks are in need of a boost. Although you've been sinking your head into mountains of work, networking and gossiping for the past few months, now is the time to give your amazing brainpower a truly earned rest.

With Mars surging into Leo on the 24th, you feel positive again about your romantic escapades. After all, you genuinely enjoy being the centre of attention, so why not cast all doubts aside and enjoy a whirl of sexy flirtatious activity.

July

Single or not, you'll be in the mood to enjoy some amusing escapades or romantic encounters of the very close kind before the 23rd. You're at your most flirtatious and adaptable, and with Mercury in fiery Leo from the 5th, you'll feel like making firm decisions or confirming your feelings to a lover or intimate partner. A wonderful sense of being special will put you in your most extrovert of moods, so make sure you're buzzing with parties or events. Fill up your diary and enjoy an active social calendar for the whole of July. This is the time to feel truly in harmony with your friends, lovers and work colleagues.

Venus's rift with Jupiter on the 17th, and then with Pluto on the 24th, triggers off a feeling of vulnerability where intimate relationships are concerned. It's not that others have changed the rules or even need time out for a break, but simply that there's an air of frustration, as if time has slowed down and you're passing each day and nothing's happening the way you want it to. But don't worry, use your bewitching charm to keep any lover enthralled, because this is truly a month when you don't need to prove anything.

Most of July you'll be at your most frivolous and fun-loving, and with Venus gathering strength in your own sign all month, your partner will be exuding more lust for you than ever before. Make good use of the subtle tension between Mars and Neptune on the 16th, when you'll feel like seducing your man and he just won't be able to resist. If you're single, sensitive Pisceans, fiery Leos or delicious strangers will keep you on your toes. So if you feel in a time warp and need to find a diversion to amuse your active mind, go for a long weekend away from the hustle and bustle, or simply move the bed around in true Gemini spirit and prove you're insatiable when it comes to daring sexual techniques.

August

If you're still all out of men by the 13th, divert your eyes when a weird coincidence gets you man-catching. Somehow you always manage to be in the right place at the right time and this kind of coincidental luck this month can only enhance your sex appeal. If you've got a lover, this is a new phase of wondrous sexual indulgence to really highlight your need for pleasure. Just take care you don't ask for too much and assume everyone else will fall in with your plans.

With Mercury retrograde from the 10th to the 25th, you might feel that a lover or new romance just isn't working out as you would like it to. But long-term pleasure, entertainment and romantic liaisons gradually turn to positively dreamlike affairs at the end of the month. And the Piscean Full Moon on the 30th gives you the sexiest of dreams. Now's the time to divulge a few of your fantasy secrets, so take your lover to the summit of all kinds of fun, both playful and physically erotic. There's no doubt that when you want to spill the beans you'll do it not only verbally but with the kind of virtuoso performance you're known for. You'll be in the mood for the truth, so let it flow.

With Pluto's move forward at the end of the month, you begin to enter a phase of personal transformation and that means one relationship has to adapt to your changing needs if it's going to survive.

September

If you're single, join a group of friends or colleagues for a period of brainstorming and social planning around the 3rd – you're full of creative talent and gaining recognition for it too. One hyper-sexy rogue wants to drag you away from the pack on the New Moon of the 14th to get creative with your body. You're feeling so outrageously wicked, you could show him a few tricks too. Jupiter's move into Libra on the 25th, and the saucy liaison with Mars on the 26th, brings you the most challenging yet sexiest few days of the month. Anything from new romance to the complications of a love triangle could arise, but you'll know where your heart truly lies.

It's hard making a decision about whether to give up on a relationship that has been chugging along quite easily, yet now seems static and lifeless. Carry on the way you are and you'll still wonder if Mr Perfect is waiting round the corner; split and you know you'll feel lost without companionship. But when Mercury enters Libra on the 28th, you are more rational and able to see the way forward. This is definitely a difficult but life-changing month relationship-wise, when you recognize that romance, excitement and adventure are more important than day-in, day-out routine. So what's holding you back? Grab your genie's lamp and rub hard – there's a beautiful image of your perfect partner in there. And with the coming autumnal air, commitment to your personal needs and beliefs become the most important words in your vocabulary.

At the end of this month, the Sun and Mars surge through the raunchiest area of your chart putting you at the peak of desirability and raring to satisfy your needs.

October

From the 2nd, Jupiter's ongoing presence in your romantic zone heralds dizzy moments and sensual encounters. If you're not going on your honeymoon, you're probably setting off on a very romantic jaunt with a potential new lover. This is a real month for making decisions and committing yourself to a serious double act. But don't upset the boat on the 14th, when the partial Solar eclipse makes you contradictory and argumentative. It could cause tension in an otherwise idyllic scenario, so either bite your tongue or look forward to steamy reconciliations. Luckily, unpredictable spats are great currency for delicious moments of making up. When gentle Venus links up with the Moon around the 16th, offer to kiss every part of your lover's body. Work your way past his pride and spice things up as you reach that libido centre.

Don't get sidetracked on the 28th when the Lunar eclipse brings a few twinges of doubt about losing your independence. But seductive Venus moves into Libra on the 29th and you realize that romance and freedom aren't mutually exclusive. Ignore any onlookers who mumble and grumble you're not doing the right thing, they're only envious of your romantic achievements.

November

This looks like being a free and easy, casual month ahead for you, but watch out that you don't start imagining or interpreting the wrong messages from those who are really close to you. Every Gemini has a habit of distorting other people's words and ideas because they really want to see the clearest and most vivid picture of the meaning behind the facts. It's a trait that means you get wound up into all kinds of confusion about who says what to whom and 'did he actually mean X when I thought he meant Z?' In other words, although you're in the mood to play, don't get caught out by your own deeply insecure 'behind the scenes' defence mechanism. Especially as relationships seem to be a high priority this month. You may have sorted out the sexy rogues from the anoraks recently, but quite honestly there are more enigmas in your love life now than there has been for a long time.

Although you love to be adored, you hate to feel trapped, so watch out around the 7th when a boyfriend appears to make too many demands on you. It's not that he's pushing for answers or even for results, but he may expect you to know all the answers. Actually, you usually do. Compromising and adapting is what you're good at doing, but usually you do so only when it's to suit you not other people. But don't worry, after the 9th you'll feel free-spirited again and you can look forward to greater happiness in your romantic life. By the 11th, you'll be wondering what all the fuss was about.

Conversations on a personal level with a platonic male friend could get blown up out of all proportion on the 20th, but inflated or exaggerated demands and assumptions will be so one-sided you'll spot the flaws easily in his judgement. Don't risk asking his advice until the end of the month – his confusion and unreliability could prove to be a waste of time and energy in an important personal dealing.

December

This is the time of the year when focussing on how you relate to others and how you relate to yourself takes on massive propor-tions, so don't let your plans get shelved by a lack of self-belief. Now is the time to light a match to your dreams and watch the adventure truly begin to flame.

With your ruler Mercury really forcing you to think things through after the 18th, think hard about your motives concerning a close relationship. If you are seriously committed but can't admit to your feelings, then this could be the opportunity you've been waiting for; alternatively, if the time has come to replot your rela-tionship, then take a deep breath and start again. If you're unat-tached, a romantic liaison while enjoying those pre-Christmas festivities could throw buckets of water on some old flames.

Although the month seems to be one of questioning and testing your relationships, it also ends with celebration and a financial bonus. There's an excellent boost to your income around the Full Moon on the 26th, so grab your purse and set off for your favourite sales; if you're single, you could also bump into the kind of stranger you've been dreaming about. Focus and listen to your own heart as well as the advice of others the last week of December, for whatever you hear, say or do will have important benefits for your long-term happiness. Enjoy New Year's Eve with a sizzling and socially flirtatious whirl, and look forward to a powerful and deeply meaningful year ahead of you with the kind of lover that gives you the chance to live your own life the way you truly want.

Your Love
Horoscope
2004

Cancer
The Crab

June 21 – July 20

Love Check

Why you're fabulous

- Men just can't resist your sensual aura.
- Once you include someone in your sacred personal space, you'll do so for life.
- You are totally loyal to your tribe of family, colleagues and friends.

Why you're impossible

- Your moods swing like a pendulum.
- You take things very personally and then react defensively.

Your love secrets

- You're restless, unpredictable and sexually wild.
- You're a match for any man who tries to seduce you.
- Sexually, you're very aware of what does and doesn't turn you on.

Your sexual style

Sensual, sultry and magnetic.

Who falls for you

Macho-men who want to control you or 'mummy's boys' who hunger for your warmth.

Who you fall for

Ambitious whizz kids, succesful down-to-earth business magnets, airy intellectual types and cool operators.

You identify with

Men who have a sense of family and history, dynasty or tribal law, but also emotional honesty.

Your greatest temptation

Playing the 'victim-saviour' game to win a man.

Your greatest strength

Being able to cope with all his moods as well as your own.

Your Love
Horoscope
2004

Passion Profile for 2004

You've been treading water for some time, especially in dealings with loved ones who wanted you to play a more serious role in their everyday lives. After a bout of soul-searching this January, you realize that's just what you were avoiding and ease off. With Saturn backtracking in your own sign right through until March 7, you can't work out if someone special has put up barriers to stop you from sharing your feelings. But mid-March provides blissful dreams and for the next few months you have a socially magical period, leading to a fresh start and decluttering of mental, material and emotional deadwood. Summer draws a curtain across a big emotional drama, helping you make a clean break. August brings love and luck, thanks to Venus fighting your romantic corner. But by August 10, someone will have left your domestic set-up with passions running high. Uplifting, heart-warming moments come in September, as Jupiter moves into Libra, reminding you that friends, fun and laughter are as essential as love. Making time for your personal needs becomes all important – you're integrating past experiences with future plans, and by the end of the year you will have found the confidence to take a leap of faith. Reach out and enter the mind-broadening path you've been seeking. Sit on the sidelines and you'll simply stew in ageing juices. Your future's in your hands and there really is only one way to jump – your way and forward.

2004 Month by Month

January

Don't hesitate to scoop up a lucrative romantic offer which comes your way around the Full Moon in your own sign on the 7th. Whether it's through a work contact or just an opportunity for social networking, with the Sun in your relationship zone, this is the time to begin working towards your dreams. A change to your outlook on life will bring a change within, but don't let it alter your fundamental nature. By all means become feistier in business, but if you're feistier in your love life, be gentle with people's feelings. Venus moves into Pisces after the 15th and you're working out how to cut loose from a relationship which is going nowhere. On the 18th, don't drop your guard and lose your self-respect in a moment of desire.

With Mars pressing on through Aries all month, you're launched into a new sizzling run of possible admirers if you're single. If you're attached, then you begin to realize that both of you have to work a little harder to maintain the right kind of equilibrium. By the 22nd, if you're looking for romance, not only will you be going to an unexpected candlelit dinner for two, you'll probably be organizing it. With your idealism sparkling like a beacon, you're on a mission to find Prince Charming. Audition your candidates carefully and see if they can make your toes curl. When you've found him and he takes you back to his castle, make him treat you like a princess. Single or attached, you deserve all the love and attention you can get this month, and it feels as if you're gradually finding out that however much you try to pretend to be something you're not, it's usually your own unique self that attracts the attention.

February

An expansive and adventurous phase evolves through a meeting with a delightful stranger on a journey, who becomes a sensual soulmate as you swap life stories and dreams. The Full Moon in fiery Leo on the 4th makes it highly likely you'll be swapping phone numbers too. Something in the way he floats through life without hangups draws you to him like a moth to a flame. You might be recognizing the need for freedom in yourself and have aspirations to cut the strings holding you back. Learn his way of loving, which could be as much about nurturing your own needs as those of others.

If you're attached, Mercury's swift move through Aquarius between the 7th and the 26th triggers off a few days of low self-esteem. You might think you have to be deceptive about your sexual needs and play the game your boyfriend's way, but a small ego boost on the 25th makes you imaginative and perceptive instead. And with Mars in earthy Taurus from the 3rd, you'll soon be able to voice your physical needs and feel completely free of inhibitions. Drop those expectations too, ask for nothing more than what you have here and now, and you'll be surprised at how happy and liberated you feel.

With a Piscean New Moon on the 20th, your social demands change and you want to share your new-found knowledge with your friends. When Mercury sidles up to Uranus on the 27th, your plans to meet up with someone you were convinced was once so special may well be unexpectedly delayed or postponed. But maybe that's just life's way of telling you to move on.

March

You're oozing persuasiveness and flattery gets you everywhere this month. But remember, the best form of flattery is based on reality, so create happiness amongst friends and lovers by seducing them with subtle compliments. Gentle words rather than direct action will ease relationship tensions and encourage the intimacy you crave with a deeply sensual partner around the Full Moon of the 6th. After the 8th, Venus fills you with ideas to bring beauty into your life or find it out there in the big wide world, whether you travel to an architectural wonder or just bump into a very gorgeous stranger.

Blissful days dreaming about an ex makes you realize that you need closeness and warmth, not a string of one-night stands or purely sexual affairs. But with Mercury's move into Aries on the 12th, you intuitively know what a colleague's thinking about you and it's not very professional. But don't react too soon, as Neptune's influence on the 20th makes things seem what they're not. Emotionally you manage to stay cool and you amuse yourself with the flirtatious attention. E-mail sex will make you both so aroused neither of you will be able to move from your desk because you're so wrapped up in each other's desires. But with Mars's influence on the 21st you can't stop thinking about him and wish you had more self-control. But luckily, a passing comment from a supportive friend makes you realize that it's all just a game. Learn from what's said and remember your promise to yourself earlier in the month. That sex without warmth and closeness is like champagne without the bubbles – terribly dull and flat.

April

Make the most of your seductive skills and sophisticated ways to woo the perfect partner, as the Full Moon shines its silver light onto your relationships on the 5th. Your glorious imagination is at its height around the 4th, as Venus encourages you to sing, play and laugh your way into any delectable lover's arms. You're feeling charismatic and spring is certainly in the air and in your step, so it's virtually impossible for anyone to resist. But your standards are exacting when Venus squares up to Jupiter on the 14th. You're unconsciously comparing everyone to a past lover you never quite got out of your system. And all the while, Jupiter's creating illusions and delusions about what you really want. One minute you know deep down that you need commitment and emotional security, the next you just want to be brazen and experimental. On top of it all, Mercury's stalling effects until the 30th brings sizzling tension between you and a platonic male friend. Make sure you're not deluding yourself, while your heart and loins have control of your head. Neptune makes you dream of a clandestine reconciliation with that past lover on the 25th, when one admirer becomes disappointing and you begin to think you'll never find the man of your dreams.

Around the New Moon of the 19th, you'll make a major decision which will create one important closure and many new beginnings. But your passions are undeniable this month and, as the Sun moves on through Taurus, you have to give in to them, even at the cost of someone else's feelings. By the 24th, you're at your most sensitive, so just make sure that whatever it is you want to say or do is really coming from your heart and not just what someone wants to hear.

May

With Mars entering your own sign on the 7th and supplying the fuel to spur you into action, you're determined to get one special person to notice you. By the 9th, you're on a quest to make your mark, and whether you take up the gauntlet and call them or knock them dead with your grace and charm, you're going to make the kind of impact that will never be forgotten.

You're making deep impressions on someone else without noticing it after the 17th, when Venus comes to a halt in your secret zone. Around the New Moon on the 19th, whispering explicit come-ons could be music to their ears as well as their libido. But don't commit yourself to anything which you can't back out of, as Mercury's mischievous influence scrambles lines of communication just when something or someone more potent could be round the corner. Yet you're in a wonderfully ephemeral mood and on the 16th you need to express yourself whether your current partner is willing to listen or not. Find a creative outlet away from it all, head off with your poetry book or watercolours and give yourself space to open your mind to what you truly want. A part of you very much wants to belong to someone, but you realize that that person must be worthy of your attention, care and, most of all, the real inner you.

Revealing too much of yourself feels like over-exposure this month, so play the games, love whoever comes within range and begin to understand what your true needs and desires are all about. When the Sun moves into your relationship zone next month you'll realize what they are. Let a current *amour* know this month that in no uncertain terms are you beginning to discover what love truly means for you.

June

You're at your most enigmatic this month, as the cosmos begins to acknowledge your needs and desires. You'll feel in the mood to pamper yourself and you'll want to get your home, boudoir or love nest in shape. Most people think Cancer is all about domesticity and family life, but you know there's an ambitious and highly motivated side to your love nature. What matters is that you feel a sense of continuity in your life and when you have this you can be as extrovert and dynamic as anyone else.

This month you can indulge in your wanderlust instinct and your need for variety and change in intimate relationships. Socially you'll be at your most vivacious and flirtatious. Okay, you have a very subtle way of seducing, a sexual instinct for whose chemistry blends with your own; seductive overkill is not your way. But around the 21st prove that your instincts are absolutely spot on when a chance encounter at a social or business function gives you the opportunity to make an important and highly confidential connection that is essential for your future career.

If you're attached, whisper delicious words to your lover and enjoy a new sensual togetherness on the 8th, and by the 23rd you'll be sharing your dreams with him. The dynamic sexual energy you share for the first few weeks of June carries on right until the end of the month, but both of you may need to take some deep breaths around the 24th, when Mars moves out of your sign into fiery Leo, highlighting the area of your chart concerning physical intimacy. Now you won't just be talking about your feelings, sexually you'll feel how powerful the energy is between you.

If you're single, a wonderful encounter brings an offer you can't refuse on the 8th, and by the 23rd this could be the lover of your dreams. Don't just fantasize about him – use your most bewitching enigmatic smile and let him know you're fascinated by him too. On the other hand, if you're still hankering after that key job, you could even be sharing a lift up to the top floor with someone who secretly can't resist your stunning charisma.

July

The Full Moon on the 2nd enhances intimate moments with one lover. Now is the time for truly magical sexual pleasure. If you've been feeling confused as to whether you are physically compatible or not, this is a week when you'll confirm to yourself that it's only feelings of insecurity on your part which are making you think that way. As far as he's concerned you are bliss personified. Being raised to goddess status means you can indulge in all your wildest fantasies, particularly those sexual steamy ones. If you're single, watch out for a dark horse among the bright and breezy men who literally keep popping up from the floor below, whether it's the flat beneath you or the offices in the basement. This one doesn't say much, but he's definitely got his eyes on you.

Around the 6th, you'll have an unusual craving to speak openly about your most private of feelings. Grab the opportunity to express your secret desire to a close friend or intimate, but don't let others try to convince you they know what's best for you. Frankly, you're beginning to free yourself from those impossible dreams about an ex. It's been plaguing you for some time, but although onlookers want to be supportive, they don't always have your best interests at heart, more likely their own. This is your chance to see yourself clearly – your needs, your wants and your desires – and finally make a clean break from the drama that's been haunting you. You'll be in the mood for dazzling everyone with your enthusiastic mood and you'll be enjoying your social life without him by your side. Feeling inspired and courageous, go out on the 17th while the New Moon is in your own sign and invest in a wonderful sexy new number or perfume just to give your fabulous charisma a boost. Now you'll definitely get noticed by an important new contact.

After the 26th, when Mercury starts to move forward again, analyzing your emotions rather than being judgmental and over-critical about yourself means you'll discover what will bring you the greatest happiness.

August

At the beginning of the month you have a desire for communicating all kinds of fascinating and juicy bits of gossip, and you could be up all night plotting strategies for friends and their relationships, or even running around like a lunatic from friend's places to clubs, bars and shops in a totally adaptable mood. Whatever comes your way around the 7th, thanks to Venus finally alighting seductively in your own sign, you can enjoy the pace and you know your restless nature can take it once in a while.

With Mars boosting your self-esteem after the 12th, whatever success you're anticipating, remember that when you are at your most enigmatic you are also at your most shrewd. Take advantage of an unusually affectionate male friend on the 18th – it could seem as if he's just being ultra flirtatious at a social event, but in fact he's an important contact for your secret ambitions. Don't divulge anything to him until you're sure you can trust him, but be at your most insightful and instinctive, watch his face closely, and remember that you have a tenacious need to succeed and get to the top of your profession and this contact could help you get there.

All that emotional baggage is now a thing of the past. You've dropped it and now magically your domestic scene is free of clutter too. Passions may be running high, but far better you express your anger than to deny your feelings. And you've finally split from memories of that lone wolf and it's time to move on.

Talking of luggage, the Piscean Full Moon on the 30th makes you dream of faraway places. So blow the dust off your bag and arrange a fabulous jaunt while you're in a travelling mood. Planning a short trip or a long weekend away will do wonders for your sense of vitality and your need for a complete chilling-out session. Make sure you go with a new lover or a close friend and take pleasure in a total relaxation break.

September

Take advantage of a self-centred early autumnal makeover and see what it does for your sex life, let alone your own personal sense of beauty. As Venus flows steadily on into your physical zone, you'll find not only are you now able to say what you truly feel, but you're also able to relax into your body instead of always feeling vulnerable and anxious about any lingering inhibitions. You'll also find a valuable source of advice this month – a flattering colleague who will inspire you and remind you of how much you are capable of taking on board. You can't mother everyone, but this month cherish only those who know you have the ambition and creative talent to succeed.

Some serious networking is needed now and for the next two months, as Venus energizes your brilliant interactive skills. Don't let the opportunity pass for beneficial new connections. They are out there if you make the effort to find them. With Mercury emphasizing your communication zone from the 10th through to the 28th, take advantage of a tremendous burst of energy for socializing and organization – parties just wouldn't be the same without you. You'll be in the mood for seducing every beautiful stranger you meet and you'll feel at your most charismatic and stunning. A wonderful opportunity occurs for a glamorous soiree on the 23rd, so make sure you're seen at your most shimmering and turn the heads that count.

It may seem as if relationships are running smoothly, but it's only because you've been so self-absorbed you haven't had time to notice what's going on beneath the surface. Take care, by the end of the month you realize you have to put more effort into one special relationship than you ever thought you'd have to.

October

Relationships are challenging this month, to say the least, but with the Sun moving on towards your romantic zone, get ready for a new lease of potent man-manageability. You'll be tripping over men in the street after the 17th, single or not. Your sensual aura will prove irresistible and you'll be stunning at work and at play.

If you're single, being attracted to a fiery and dynamic newcomer will send ripples of desire quivering through your body, but don't just take the first man you meet – hunt your pleasure with true

Cancerian sensitivity. You'll be totally surprised by your own reactions and responses, always so finely tuned to the environment. So ensure you hunt well.

If you're already hooked, together you'll discover a new and exciting sexual dynamism. So lavish him with love and sex and you'll enter a new phase of deep emotional trust and intimacy, just what you've been waiting for. How could you have survived without it?

The Lunar eclipse on the 28th puts you in an extrovert mood and you'll be dancing or making love from dawn to dusk if given the chance. Meanwhile, enjoy and delight in some girlie giggling over a romeo who thinks he can make out with everyone on the work front. Some hilarious entertainment will energize your libido and your enigmatic aura will inspire one special person to want you, and only you.

November

After the 11th, thanks to Mars rocketing on into your romantic zone, you'll be at your most sensual and you'll have a feeling that horizons are opening up and life is really buzzing. There is a sense of constancy now in your personal life but also a need to keep changing, keep moving, keep the flow of your life shifting in rhythm with your feelings.

Around the 14th, be prepared for an exciting and unexpected confirmation of all your deepest sexual desires. Now you can reach deeper into your heart and steer the course of an intimate relationship in the direction you truly crave. Take care though if you feel confused about a boyfriend's feelings or needs – trust in yourself and by nurturing the dream of romantic happiness, remember you can make it become a reality.

The New Moon in sexy Scorpio on the 12th means you could now be ready to open some new doors to emotional happiness and personal stability. However much you put on a show to cover up your feelings, Venus's influence after the 22nd will bring you closer to revealing to yourself that your emotions are churning around this month for no better reason than you must attend to them or at least share them with your partner. With so much pleasure and happiness around you, look to the darker days of winter as a chance to feast on your feelings rather than agonizing over why you keep changing your moods and your mind.

Loving yourself will be easy for the last week of November and as Uranus, the planet of electrifying sex, now moves forward again through the area of your chart concerned with transformation and sexuality, you'll feel ready for a deeper rapport with your lover. Even if it leads to a change in your lifestyle or awakens you to a decision about whether this is the right man for you, what matters is your rejuvenated self-esteem – and November steams you sauna-fulls.

December

You've had so many headaches concerning work issues recently December sees luck and pleasure finally paying attention to you. With the Sun moving into the area of your chart concerning romance, pleasure and fun on the 21st, you can now begin to relax and take time out to enjoy the company of those who truly mean something to you, rather than be swallowed up by the rat race or pre-Christmas organization. The beginning of December, however, sees a brief testing time with one special person before you can seriously get down to having a good time. On the 2nd, you come to terms with why he doesn't seem to know whether he's coming or going. And it could just be that somehow you're not communicating what you truly feel or think. Outbursts abound, but use your gentle and serene ability to avoid causing a mindless conflict of interests.

As a Moon-ruled Water sign, you need to feel secure in your relationships before you give too much of yourself away, so take precautionary steps to ensure you're spending the first few days of December in the calmest and most tranquil of locations, with time to reflect. However much you mean to someone, and however much you love to dream of complete happiness, you still know deep down inside that you have a shifting, changing nature – a weather map all of your own, which sometimes few others understand. But particularly this month it's important for you to realize that finding warmth and moving with your changing moods and feelings is not a contradiction as others might want you to believe.

Always in tune to the rhythms of the Moon, you could have to make compromises around the Full Moon in your own sign on the 26th, which highlights the need to verify whether you're sabotaging your relationship because you daren't commit for fear of rejection. If you're single, take the chance to improve a relationship with someone who at first seems an unlikely candidate for your future long-term happiness, but who could turn out to be the catalyst for all your dreams to come true. An off-the-cuff conversation around the 30th restores your self-belief and gives you the confidence to re-plot love's mysterious workings for the new year.

Your Love
Horoscope
2004

Leo

The Lion

July 21 – August 21

Love Check

Why you're fabulous

 Glamorous, fun-loving and sizzling with energy, you are every man's best friend.

 Men adore your flamboyant sexual style.

 You are totally loyal and committed when you know your man is too.

Why you're impossible

 If you can't have your way you'll throw yourself on the floor in a tantrum.

 You loathe being ignored and have to be the centre of attention.

Your love secrets

 You'd love to be attached to someone famous.

 Sexually, you are inexhaustible and love to dominate.

 If your man doesn't tell you he loves you every day you sulk.

Your sexual style

 Dramatic, showy and direct.

Who falls for you

 Pleasure-loving rogues who want someone glamorous hanging on their arm. Down-to-earth rugged types who are spellbound by your show-stopping performance.

Who you fall for

 Men who make you feel 'number one' and are equally numb with admiration. Eccentrics, intellectuals and mavericks, or men who run up impressive expense account lunches without batting an eyelid.

You identify with

 Luxury, stylish clothes, glamorous men, celebrities and champagne breakfasts. Being the queen bee at your own party or the social lioness about town.

Your greatest temptation

 Exhibitionist sex!

Your greatest strength

 Loyalty to your man – whatever he has to put up with, so will you.

Passion Profile for 2004

Mars's surge into Aries this January opens your eyes to the surprising affects you have on the opposite sex and by June, when the feisty potent planet moves on into your own sign, you're promised mystery admirers, whirlwind romances and love triangles, so prepare for a sizzling summer. A year of drama, glamour and excitement beckons, as the celestial line-up makes it difficult to differentiate between real feelings and superficial ones. But you're heading for such a roller-coaster ride you have to expect a few bumps along with the thrills. By December, the thrills will have been many and you'll end the year on a romantic high. Only you know if you'll be married by Christmas, but you'll enjoy being in the spotlight, and isn't that just how you like it?

2004 Month by Month

January

Spurred on by the courage and the will never to be defeated in love, you will be entering a more dramatic and resolute new year regarding your relationships. Work ambitions have kept you busy and more excited about your future than anything else early in the month, but at the end of January career issues play havoc with your love life. You want time for both work and love, but sometimes the two just don't mix.

With Mars's influence all month, you have an endless string of admirers everywhere you go and your mobile phone is filled with enticing names and numbers. You're still heady with one sexual involvement of a kind you hadn't expected around the New Moon on the 21st and you begin to suspect that emotion has more to do with your new-found sexual activity than pure lust.

Around the 24th, expect a few arguments and a build-up of tension on the home front. Friends will antagonize you because they're frustrated by your impulsive actions. They may even resent one of your more escapist love affairs – or simply your renewed passion for yourself and being the central figure in everyone else's love stories. When you're thoroughly involved with someone in a fling such as this, you carry the air of the great Houdini – you love every moment of the danger of commitment it brings, but you always know there is a way out if you feel too trapped or suffocated.

Work pressures will make any affair of the heart difficult to sustain this month, or you might find you exclude friends for the interest of one special *amour*. Temporary distance from a partner is beneficial around the 14th, when Venus conjuncts Uranus, because one such relationship might suffer from the strain of your ambitious streak, when you're in the mood for wanting everything now.

February

Competing with rivals, or simply being challenged by love, is one of the most exciting ways you are turned on this month. The fire and impetus in your aims won't be repressed and you'll come bouncing back with a stronger will and a more resolute desire to find that perfect relationship.

You may lose a friend to another group this month, thanks to the sacrificial effect of the New Moon on the 20th. But once people see that you're forever the champion of passion and imagination in your love life, others will begin to respect your sense of integrity and realize that when love's at stake you will play the game for all it's worth.

Physically, you'll feel high-spirited and full of enthusiasm for a busy and active sex life. Your ruling Sun glows in Pisces after the 19th, a sexually driven area of your chart, where you will feel one minute enchanted by all the choice on offer, the next compelled to become more involved with one lover above all others. With a wonderful Full Moon earlier in the month in Leo on the 6th, by the 26th you will feel as close to someone and as free as you want to at the same time. The very independence you seek can be found in a partner who understands the motivation behind your impulse and drive. And probably another Fire sign, like Aries or Sagittarius, could come into your life and it will be hard to keep them out. Defiant though you can be if you feel sexually restricted, you also want some kind of commitment and loyalty. By the 26th, you have a sneaky suspicion that the two aren't mutually exclusive. If you're already involved in a very deep relationship, your loyalty might be in question, when you're tempted by a brief and challenging romantic encounter around the 27th.

March

With so much emphasis in your chart of planets in Air and Fire signs this month, you feel emotionally on a high and challenged by more than your fair share of risk-taking or dare-devil romantic escapades. This may encourage you to go out and about, to seek the pleasures of more than your usual haunts and parties, and, if you're single, to travel further afield in your search for romance. With Mercury moving into Aries on the 12th, followed by the Sun and a New Moon on the 20th, you just can't have enough of some-one's very stimulating company. They may not be a knight in shin-ing armour, but they do have class, style and a good heart, so don't take advantage of them without giving a little back.

Your pioneering instinct is strong all month and, like last month, you feel one minute trapped, the next that you have the freedom of the open road. You will view any emotional territory that is un-familiar to you with suspicion, but with Mars in Gemini, you're feeling optimistic about your romantic ideals and your theatrical flair and nose for drama puts you in the limelight all month. After the 21st, your ruling Sun gives you the chance to shine at all the best social dos and parties. Frankly, you're in the mood to dazzle and seduce all those sexy admirers. It's time to be the protagonist in your own romantic film. Especially as one handsome rogue is up for playing the supporting role. Just take care around the 30th when he innocently flirts with a friend and you want to control his life. Don't take it personally or you could end up under the spotlight, alone.

April

If you're single, the deeper sexual intimacy you crave with an admirer begins to be more viable this month. He's more conscious of your needs, more accepting of your independence, and is beginning to trust in you enough to realize you'll be the most loyal and devoted lover yourself.

As much as Mercury's retrograde movement through Taurus between the 5th and the 30th might undermine your attempts to have it out with one partner, the subtler effects of Venus's links with Uranus on the 8th and Jupiter on the 14th will lead to clarity about your mutual differences. It might feel like there's a black cloud on the horizon on the 4th when your partner just doesn't want to give up someone or something else in his life just for you. Then the following week you'll have heard it all from a pal about why love isn't just about romantic adventure and there's more to it than that. Who do you believe? Who do you trust? Remember, you need fire, passion and endless fantasies for the future and any down-to-earth criticism of the way you love is frankly going to make you even more determined to have things your way. As much as you're governed by your desires, your instincts are always spot on, and with the New Moon on the 19th, trust in your psychic sense more than that well-meaning friend who thinks she knows romantically what's best for you.

The illuminating aspect between Mars and Jupiter on the 4th is the instigator of all your excessive behaviour and motivated desires, and by the end of the month you realize that your prime objective in your emotional life is not only about where you are going, but who it is you know can walk alongside you, with pride, belief and respect for your passion for living. Check them out carefully.

May

At last you have the courage to express yourself more openly and more dramatically than you have for a long time. Not that you were ever lacking courage but just you didn't feel you could ever find the right moment to speak up. Your needs are unequivocal this month and that's what a lover or partner has to hear, however much he might try to blind himself from the truth. Emotionally you may falter, but if you take the chance to air your doubts and fears about where a relationship is going and whether you want it to go any further, at least it will give him insight into your true motives and beliefs at last. Instead of insisting you know best, you could find that he takes the initiative and goes his separate way for a few days around the 17th. With Venus's backtracking motion until the end of June, you can't be sure of anything. So give him his space, as much as you want it for yourself. A test in love can only show how secure or how rocky love is anyway. And in the meantime you can find out if you're also sure about this particular romance working or going any further.

With Mars moving into Cancer on the 7th, you feel as if you're having to give up more than you want, or perhaps others are blaming you for relationships not working. But this is a month for calm reflection, self-analysis and a little fun between all that hard work. Essentially, if you follow the path you've always taken, then you can be sure that love won't end just because you have ambivalent feelings right now. Nor will anyone else stop loving you because you aren't the life and soul of every party. Sometimes even you need to chill out.

June

The Full Moon on the 3rd makes you crave an evening of self-indulgent pampering so you can enjoy looking your fabulous best for the rest of June. The 15th is a busy day for family connections and by the 21st you'll be in social demand over and over again. The New Moon on the 17th casts an extrovert glow around you and you'll be at your most charismatic. So take the opportunity to stand out in the crowd, so those with true prestige and influence can see your leadership ability in a new light. Watch out for a rival or competitor who tries to take the spotlight or your man away from you. Be smart and take care you remain your usual cool, glamorous and impeccable self. By the end of the month you'll be in the mood to shine at every party or social event, so accept every invitation – the more visible you make yourself, the more successful you will become, especially if you're still looking for that perfect partner.

Certain personal issues are still at the back of your mind and there have been times, you must admit, when you'd rather forget about them and get on with the fun side of Leo life. However, resolving your most personal problems takes precedence this month and it's time to press ahead and face up to the facts. Do so after the 24th, when Mars rockets into your own sign, and you're suddenly more assertive, challenging and prepared to stand up for your own needs and desires. Don't fear you will be rejected for being true to your individuality. If you are, then someone doesn't really love the real you, just the image they have of how you should be. And is that true love? Hardly. Free of worries and blessed with growing self-esteem, you can make new arrangements and commitments that matter without burning yourself out nor denying yourself the right to be you.

July

With fiery Mars still in your own sign, followed by Mercury on the 5th, you begin to feel sexually alight and full of dramatic and passionate desire. Drag your new or current man into a luscious bedroom scenario and he'll be spellbound. This is now a time when you can both learn to express your feelings and communicate your sexual needs and pleasures. You know as a Leo you need to dominate and to make the decisions, but being in charge could prove more complicated around the 16th, when Mars's wrangle with Neptune makes your man make a few hasty decisions of his own. Tame him back to your intensely individualistic ways on the 24th, when Venus and Pluto give you the power of sexual persuasion. A sultry seduction number or a dramatic and outrageous sexual scenario will lull him into desire and passion for you instantly, and he'll remember that you are the one who needs self-recognition and the one who needs to be needed.

If you're single, an unexpected encounter this month promises the ultimate in Leo love. You'll feel independent, seductive and dynamic enough to stage your performance with absolute enthusiasm, so turn the tables on him and really enjoy the art of dramatic passion.

August

Celebrate the Sun's ongoing influence in your sign until the 22nd, bringing good fortune to every aspect of your life, and it seems like you're the most charismatic seductress on the planet. The succession of eager admirers confirms that you are. Hot-headed followers won't stop ringing and e-mailing for dates. With all the attention it probably will go straight to your head. But if it's your birthday, shouldn't you be allowed a little treat? Indulge your spicy flirtations in a 'smackerel' of Leo loving, but watch out if you're already emotionally involved, the jealousy could prove too much for someone to bear. By the Leo New Moon of the 16th, your passions are unquenchable and you're ready to indulge in anyone who truly deserves your loving arms – just make sure if you're single that you make the right choice. There is a chance you'll feel as if you made a really big mistake come the dawn.

After the 10th, Mars moves on into Virgo to give you huge reserves of sensual energy. Direct this energy carefully and don't let your mind and body run too wild around the 20th, when you're considering pushing sexual boundaries. Listen to your instincts and discover the sexual equivalent to the pot of gold at the end of the rainbow. It'll be glistening with the light of the gentle Full Moon in your sexual zone on the 30th, bringing opportunities for tender but fervent adoration.

September

Hot and spicy conversations abound on the 6th between you and a boyfriend, so enjoy the passion. But it could seem as if he's more interested in working out the next few months of his life than any deeper intention towards you. Actually he's suddenly enlightened by your relationship and secretly yearns to make a closer commitment. Fear of rejection often appears in three forms: one, a cool retreat; two, a mask of indifference; three, over-possessiveness and jealousy. If he's acting out any of these then you'll know he's actually far more vulnerable than he seems to be. If you're craving a closer connection then ask yourself what it is you need to express or experience to enable the relationship to move forward. With Venus highlighting your own sign from the 6th onwards, intimate moments become more satisfying after the 18th and you realize that giving him an honest expression of your feelings is the ultimate way forward for total and complete fulfilment.

If you're single, an unexpected encounter around the 6th takes you to the outer limits of desire when a charming rogue bumps into you on the stairs. You're convinced this is one of those fated attractions when he asks you out on a date. Take care if you're easily bedazzled by flattery, this man finds you sexually irresistible, but if you're up for a fling, then don't hesitate to give him your phone number.

October

Loving and passionate as you are, you sometimes feel insecure if your loyalty isn't returned. With Neptune taking a quiet nap in your romance and relationship zone until the 24th, there's a dreamy look in a boyfriend's eye, so catch him alone and prove you're the sexiest woman since Marilyn Monroe, particularly when he's around. If you're single, you are still dreaming about that charmer you met last month, sneakily hoping he could be a long-term prospect. But it all gets very frustrating when you realize he's already involved with someone else. But do you wait for him to cut ties, just on the off chance that he's seriously interested in some kind of commitment? Or are you kidding yourself about his true motives? Don't assume too much; after all, there are other players out there if you're single, and if you're already attached then you'll be living dangerously.

Early on this month you discover one platonic friendship isn't quite as awkward and disruptive as you thought, and although you're convinced this man wants more than conversation and friendship, by the 25th you have a magical change of heart and accept that maybe you were wrong to doubt him. Well, like any Leo you love surprises and around the Solar eclipse of the 14th changes will come in your relationships which won't be so tiring and complex.

November

With Mars in Scorpio from the 11th, a release of sexual energy will feel good but intensely addictive. It might even spill over into someone's life who wasn't exactly expecting it. And with Venus also moving on into the torrid watery sign on the 22nd, your whole sexual relating could be subject to change when you least expect it. There could be undercurrents of disturbances and feelings which are not in your control and various emotions you might also wish not to express. But with the Sun moving on into Sagittarius on the 21st, you'll be able to focus with true clarity on why your feelings and sexuality work so well together. Without your ego, you wouldn't survive the desire that courses through your veins, and libido highs or not, you need to cherish your sense of self – it's the most valuable and important thing for you this month.

Boyfriends prove to be petulant and demanding throughout the month and you can't really be sure if all that fire and brimstone – the romance and passion you so desperately need – is actually going to be sustainable where one lover is concerned. It's not that you want to break up, just make life more exciting. No routine domesticity for you – if he can't understand you need to live a theatrical life, then maybe he doesn't truly understand or believe in you.

On the 14th, a sudden flurry of work responsibilities takes your mind off those relationship problems. But around the 29th, Jupiter's collusion with Neptune brings out the rebel in you and you're in the mood to say, 'It's my way, or not at all!'. Push your boyfriend too hard and the resulting fireworks and drama could be just what you were hoping for. But think carefully: are you simply out to prove you're the only power behind your relationship throne, or is it mutual passion for the same things in life that you really want?

December

Feelings this month are about loyalty and trust. Being true to yourself is second nature to you, but you could feel a few moments of self-doubt creeping in around the 15th when someone special forces you to reconsider what is really going on in your heart. It's not exactly a test of will or of you having to make compromises, only a really important sense of what truly matters to you. Ask yourself whether your need for mutual respect and honesty isn't exactly as openly discussed or acknowledged as you might like it to be. Once the feelings and the air clears you'll be set for a wonderful end to December.

Venus is highlighting your romantic relationships from the 16th and you can finally relax and enjoy the closeness and feelings of warmth and loyalty that keep you alive and vibrant. Sexually, your closest relationship will be transformative and totally indulgent around the Christmas break, as long as you make sure to remember to get him a present rather than worrying about whether he's actually got one for you. The New Moon on the 12th puts you in the mood for an intimate romantic dinner for two, even though you'd rather be out and about and seen at all the best parties. This is a time to reconnect to your truly romantic spirit, simply because your inspiration and ability to enjoy yourself will bring much happiness to someone who may not have the same self-awareness as you.

The end of December for you is about chasing up on those real emotional dreams rather than endless rainbows. Courage and motivation are the two words you need to remember as you enter the new year with fresh conviction and self-esteem. And at last you know that the excitement and desire you have for one person is now a reality, not just a vague inkling or an unfulfilled longing. You can make it work, and it's time to listen seriously to what your inner voice is saying.

Your Love
Horoscope
2004

Virgo
The Virgin

August 22 – September 22

Love Check

Why you're fabulous

 Thriving on the world of words, you can get your message across to any man.

 You care about your body image and always look impeccable.

 That virtuous smile hides a very wicked libido.

Why you're impossible

 You are quick to point out your man's flaws or mistakes.

 Bragging about how knowledgeable you are drives him mad.

Your love secrets

 You're a dreamer when your man's not there and not as down-to-earth and practical as you make out.

 You won't make love to him if he's got dirty fingernails.

 If you have a man you worship, you'd wash his socks for him.

Your sexual style

Earthy, sensual, magical and timed to perfection.

Who falls for you

Lazy men who know how efficient you are around the house. Dynamic, fiery extroverts who adore your down-to-earth sense of humour and love of sensual pleasure.

Who you fall for

Men who know the difference between yoghurt and fromage frais. Hard-working types who have stamina and adore routine and ritual, or romantic dreamers who you can organize.

You identify with

Workaholics, dieticians and men who look after their bodies. Keep-fit regimes, organic food and wholesome loving.

Your greatest temptation

Spending all day in bed with him instead of going to work.

Your greatest strength

Dedication to his sensual needs.

Passion Profile for 2004

You are stunningly persuasive this year with Jupiter in your own sign until September and partnerships are seductive and exciting. Professional success increases your pulling power through spring, but Mercury's stalling effects throughout April alters the way you view coupledom. Much as you hate relying on others, you realize you can only shoulder so much responsibility single-handedly. In late June, emotional togetherness improves through the sharing of responsibilities and goals. By July, you're being objectively positive and Venus gives you scorching ideas for seductive games and tricks. Jupiter's vivacious influence throughout the summer heralds a very sexy holiday romance if you're single or a more relaxed attitude if you're attached. Mars takes over in your own sign in August making you realize that you can no longer just pay lip service to your personal needs, you must kiss your own reflection and love yourself for who you are. Self-belief is everything as you run up to the end of the year. With it you can rule your world of relationships, without it you're destined to the rat race. You're not totally in the hands of fate – with a little awareness and self-knowledge you can improve your lot and your love life. This is your year to do so.

2004 Month by Month

January

Arousing moments abound as Jupiter enhances the sexiest area of your chart from the 2nd, promising plenty of bedroom action. The Sun and Venus boost your libido until the 6th and enthuse you with sensual ideas to satisfy you and your lover, so don't waste any time making the most of the steamy energy. By the Full Moon of the 7th, the phone won't stop ringing, bringing opportunities for a regular feast of arousal if you're single, right through until the 15th when sensible Saturn urges you to be cautious.

You're not the sort of person to squander career success for physical pleasure, so spend some time concentrating on your aspirations rather than trying to seduce or flirt in the hope you'll gain both your lover's attention and greater opportunities. It's not that you're a social climber, but you do have moments when the thought of a secret love tryst is very tempting. But you're back down on planet earth by the 18th and the Sun's move into Aquarius on the 21st fills you with so much hope and enthusiasm no-one can hold you back. You're destined to travel far, but the pressure will be on around the 24th. Goals rather than intimate discussions become strangely important, and with Venus and Mercury's influence around the 31st, you could charm bananas from the hands of monkeys. And that kind of relationship success is very sexy.

February

Enthusiasm for adventure or a brilliant new scheme gives you oodles of opportunities to meet new friends and enlighten strangers with your hopes and ideas. Their positive reaction inspires you to forge ahead and make firm plans. Excellent business partnerships are formed from the 3rd, when Mars steams on into sensual

Taurus. But if it's sexual pleasures you're angling for, make arrangements with one new love interest around the fiery Full Moon of the 6th. Head off into the sun and absorb all the new, exciting things you come across. Bright colours, dappled light and delicious smells enrich your need for beauty and inspire you to adopt a more ephemeral way of being.

By opening yourself up to new experiences, you attract a string of gorgeous admirers and tempting offers. Take up the one most in tune with your mindset and enjoy sensuous nights of passion after Valentine's Day, teaching each other what turns you on. A gentle touch and soothing words will ease pressures and get you centred on the complete enhancement of your mutual pleasure.

Around the 19th the Sun moves into Pisces and all that romantic talk does sound blissful but you realize that you can't always have your cake and eat it. The stirring link between Mercury and Uranus on the 27th gives you an unfounded sense of inadequacy which you mustn't give in to. Dig deep into your unconscious – you are strong, bright and gorgeous, you know where you're going and self-doubt has no place in your life. Dump it and shine.

March

Playing sardines on the tube, bus or train gets you noticed by someone who regularly rides your route and wants to know you better. But you're so wrapped up in personal ambitions you're too busy to realize when someone's flirting. As you're most likely considering a major new career change around the Full Moon of the 6th, that's fair enough, but Saturn's move forward again in Cancer on the 7th should encourage you to react with increased enthusiasm. Then it's up and down again. On the 9th, you're feeling baffled and communicating your feelings and desires becomes difficult. In fact, so many planets are in the aspirational part of your chart you might be best off sticking to work after all. And work can become fun – if one of your juicier colleagues begins an e-mail flirtation.

The Sun moves on into the deeply emotional part of your chart on the 20th and turns your attention to making a success out of one serious relationship that you might have neglected recently. Mercury lightens things up again on the 31st, making clear, honest communication a must, whether it's with a truly long-term partner who just needs to know where you both stand, or if all that e-mail flirting has got dirty, now is the time to spell out exactly what you'd like to do with your on-line sex partner. Whether you act it out is up to him – well, once he's recovered from the shock of seeing your sexual fantasies listed in glorious black and white.

April

Speak up about your most unusual or creative plans and ideas on the 3rd, but be prepared for someone special to attempt to seduce you into changing your allegiance, or at the very least expecting you to be tempted into a crazy office outing. Your own ruler Mercury turns retrograde from the 5th to the 30th, so quietly and purposefully get down to establishing your own motives and moves for the rest of the year. You know you want to make changes – big crazy changes – and there's a niggly feeling that you have no choice but to be realistic about a shift of emphasis in your romantic goals and ambitions too. This month you'll feel a sense of awakening, as if at last someone says the key word which triggers your whole change in attitude to yourself and your future. Watch out though you don't make any hasty moves mid-month concerning your most personal of feelings. That very special someone seems to be acting negatively towards your future ideals, so make sure you focus on evaluating their motives rather then believing you are solely to blame for their disapproval. By the end of the month you'll prove your analysis of their confusion was right.

With Venus energizing the area of your chart concerning your dedication to your self-esteem, you could feel as if you have to make rash changes concerning your romantic plans. But don't worry, this won't last if you direct your energies to ensuring your image is impeccable and remembering that you deserve love just by virtue of being. Throw a party after the 25th and enjoy the feeling of being adored by your man, or singled out for a date if you're free. Once your ruler Mercury starts beetling forward again next month, you'll be adored for your sensitivity and compassion for others, and you'll feel motivated enough to redefine and reconsider your love life. Enjoy this wonderful mood of vivacious energy and enjoyment for living.

May

This is a month for sheer dedication to your future personal happiness. If you're single, there's always a feeling that if you let slip the knowledge that you do have deep insecurities and a lot more self-doubt than anyone could ever imagine, you'll be left stranded and abandoned at the starting post. Any offers of dates are scary early on in the month, simply because you're not sure if you can maintain your poised self-confidence while you're feeling so insecure. But by the 25th you're more philosophical and one male friend confesses he has the same worries about life and love as you do. Together you realize that this could develop into a long-term rapport. Take it easy, it's worth working at.

If you're already attached, think carefully about the best way to express your fears and worries, particularly as around the 10th you panic that your lover doesn't care. It's not that your man doesn't love you, he does, but he's just thinking hard about the actual role he plays in your life. Even if he seems ambivalent, give him a chance to get things sorted out in his mind before you leap to any conclusions. Punishing yourself and him because you're not 'talking things through' in the way 'mature people' are supposed to do won't makes things any easier. There are times when you both need space, so find it, then exchange words around the 14th. You might even find you've both got exactly the same thoughts.

Nervous moments abound when Venus backtracks through your chart from the 17th and your partner begins to make extraordinary noises about how he isn't sure if this is the right way forward for your relationship. Don't worry, by the 29th things will be the way you want them to be again. It's only a matter of misunderstanding rather than incompatibility that makes you both feel so tense. By the end of the month you'll be thinking, 'What was all the fuss about anyway?'

June

Social fun isn't the only pleasure you'll have this month. If you're single, romance will be in the air after the 6th, so while out socializing have a frolic and grab that man who's drooling over you. Organize some parties or cool soirees yourself around the New Moon night of the 17th or take a quick weekend break in a romantic location by the sea, or Paris, if you've saved well last month, or simply just stay at your own place. You need social variety and with Jupiter's link-up with Venus on the 19th you'll be in the mood for travelling. Remember, if you're single that could also increase your chances for romantic encounters. Concoct some aphrodisiacs, and with Venus and Mars's help on the 24th, work on those enticing Virgoan seductive arts and hypnotize that man with your cool charisma. Tip: try a glass of cold, cold champagne or a dash of brandy poured over a sugar cube – he'll be hooked.

If you're attached, spontaneous sexual pleasure will be high on your agenda this month, and you'll feel relaxed and your relationship rekindled or improved by your new sense of self-possession. Take this month as a starting point for a more positive approach to your role in any intimate relationship. Thanks to Jupiter's influence, it's suddenly dawning on you that you're beginning to feel more emotionally in tune with your lover. Any new opportunities and goals are shared and you relax and find more time for exploring mutual needs rather than worrying about what the future holds. You don't have to be anything other than yourself to enjoy being adored. Maintain your individuality and true love will be all around you.

July

At last you're more positive about the future than you've been for a long time and increasingly you're looking at love and life through a more objective lens. Venus makes you feel cheeky and spontaneous all month and you flirt, play and delight wherever you go. But watch out for an unpredictable and provocative encounter around the 14th. It's not that you're in need of any more drama in your life than you already have, but this could be your chance to show your rivals what you are truly made of.

If you're attached, watch out for sparks flying everywhere in your relationship except where you want them to go. Relationship tiff or a more important confrontation? Whatever the consequences, let the fire die down before you jump to any hasty conclusions. Be courageous and stick to your instincts; an apology isn't necessary, but understanding is. And remember, your heart is always the true barometer for the feelings behind any dispute. It takes more than a conflict of interests or of intention to stop you from enjoying a deeply trusting relationship. If this is a new *amour*, then it could prove to be the most exciting and challenging of meetings. Any rendezvous with a dynamic and fiery opponent is always good for your ego – it stimulates your need for a flamboyant love life and reminds you that although on the surface you're cool, self-possessed and down-to-earth, beneath that sophisticated image you have a deep-seated need for passion. So be inspired and take the energy as enlivening rather than belittling.

With so much activity in the pleasure area of your chart this month, at least you won't be short of social whirls and entertaining nights. By the 18th, the social scene really hots up and you'll feel the centre of attention. Someone's secret admiration for your talent around the 22nd throws you well and truly into the limelight, so if you're trying to make an impression, wear the plunging neckline.

The last week of July looks set to be a period when clarity about your journey for the next few months will be crystal clear. So enjoy dazzling your *amour* with your spirit and self-confidence, because the future holds more happiness than you have yet dared to imagine.

August

With so much planetary activity in your own sign this month you're at your most logical and rational, and you're armed with insight and compassion regarding someone special's true feelings. But with all your intrigues and secrets you could also be surprising close relatives or intimate friends with more than their fair share of gossip. After the 7th, if you're single, you could be up for a scorching holiday romance, and if you're attached, passion gets very steamy in those sultry summer nights.

Keep an open mind this month as to what is actually relevant in your life and what isn't, particularly with regard to your own sexual needs. By the 22nd, you're relaxed and ready for a summer social whirl – and you're looking your most fabulous. Be prepared for feelings of intense romance around the Full Moon of the 30th; your mood could open you up to a distinctly clandestine possibility if you're single, or a more profound connection with your boyfriend if you're attached.

You have some great ideas for a lifestyle change around the 9th, but you're worried about expressing them because you might cause a scene with your lover. Be daring and take the opportunity to reveal your heart's desire. The dreams you have are viable and realistic, and if you can't be honest about what you want, then it will only breed resentment later. By the 19th, you'll be wondering why you ever doubted your own intuition. You are not only in the mood to dance and to be at your most seductive, but you're also finally ready to reveal your thoughts. Avoiding your feelings is the last thing to do as the days begin to shorten. And as the Sun moves into your own sign after the 22nd and clarifies what your lover really wants from you, so do your visions for a better emotional future begin to sow their seeds. Now you can be self-assured, confident and totally committed to your own direction in life, with or without him. With Mars energizing your sign all month, take every opportunity to shimmer in style and communicate your greatest hopes and schemes while you have the chance.

September

You know you need harmony, constancy and romance in your life – ideally, for you, life is about maximizing your credibility and urge for success, but also about doing so in a simply beautiful way. The rapport and atmosphere of your love life is about equilibrium and harmony, and if you don't have this you don't always feel as if you're getting anywhere. It's time, therefore, to trust in your judgement this month and confront a personal misunderstanding that you've been avoiding. Okay, it's easier to avoid making decisions and let others set the flow and the pace. However, the first week of September is a time when you could feel forced to open up and reveal more than you had anticipated. Avoiding scenes and conflicts is essential; but remember, if any do occur they won't last forever. Every mood changes and usually every conflict gets resolved. Be positive and be at your most sophisticated and calm, and you'll realize that those anxieties and confusions are now ready to leave you well and truly behind.

With a New Moon in your own sign on the 14th and your ruler Mercury giving you the voice and the confidence to speak your mind, one special lover won't be able to resist you. There's a deeper truth between you now developing, so don't fall into the 'blame game' or act out the 'saviour/victim' scenario just because you both fear being yourselves.

October

You begin to realize this month that saving money gives you a great sense of security, but then when you spend it you feel guilty. The way you handle your relationships is a bit like your cash flow this month. Friends seem more dependent on you for advice than usual and you're not sure whether you should be more generous with your time. But then if you give too much of yourself you worry that you're missing out on your own needs. And what of relationships? You know that the most important thing is to be loved and to love, and this month you can be assured of plenty of opportunities for new romance if you're single, or a deeper and closer bond with a boyfriend if you're attached.

A high-spirited liaison intensifies after the 3rd if you're attached, and you'll be ready to let someone see the real you by the 18th. If you're looking for love and romance, make sure you get out and about around the 14th – you'll be feeling at your most stunning, so accept every invite that comes your way and attend every party or event. The chances are that an exciting romantic encounter could give you the feeling of being awakened to a new adventure, so take the chance and prove to yourself that you're not just pleasing others but seriously pleasing yourself too.

With Venus blazing through your own sign from the 3rd, you'll feel like making an impact on the world. You'll be at your most seductive, so choose your words with care in all conversations regarding your future aims and you'll be sure to get what you want. Romantic offers will come to you in the most receptive and magical of ways. You experience exotic encounters in local haunts, dreamy protagonists call when you least expect and a run of dates with new blood in your professional life puts a wicked smile on your face. This is a month for renewed conviction in your own self-worth.

November

An unfulfilled need for deeper intimacy or a desire for the best life's got to offer urges you to strut your stuff and show the world you mean business, as Mars cracks a very sexy whip in Scorpio after the 11th. The New Moon of the 12th helps you discover the power you have within you and how you can actually make things happen just the way you want them to when you're feeling instinctive and intuitive. With the Sun and Mercury in the idealistic area of your chart, you'll be able to communicate to someone special that you want to spend more time with them. Take the opportunity to also let them know your sexual needs and show that you're irrepressible right now.

Thanks to Mars's dynamic influence, you just want to crusade on the behalf of everyone else. And while you're one of life's success stories, it's wholly likely that if you're single you'll fall for the underdog in the workplace. Of course he'll be a highly talented and gorgeous underdog, but nevertheless he'll need your sound advice and career guidance. Mars drives you to introduce him to useful contacts, but make sure that your trust isn't abused, when Venus moves into Scorpio on the 22nd, enhancing romantic intrigues and mischief-making.

The celestial line-up drags sex kicking and screaming into the equation by the 29th. And whether you're still with that wonder man of a few months back or involved in a delightfully spicy relationship with someone new, Mercury's standstill on the 30th demands that you drop a few of those emotional boundaries to let love in. Honour the fact that it's the only way it can enter, lower the drawbridge and discover how outrageously naughty you can be when aroused by at least one man of your dreams, even if the love is not destined to last forever.

December

The ghost of Christmas past comes back to haunt you this month and a very sexy ghost he is too. But is an ex always going to be an ex? You're feeling nostalgic around the New Moon of the 12th and it's hard to maintain social graces when you see him across a crowded Christmas party. With Mercury backtracking until the 20th, you can't stop yourself wondering if you should have split up. The problem is highlighted again on the 16th and you're lured into thinking that you'll never meet anyone quite like him again and whether you should consider taking him back. Luckily, bountiful Venus holds a mirror up to reflect the truth. Things are never what they seem through the sepia-haze of time and Venus reminds you of the things which separated you in the first place. With the Sun moving into your idealistic and romantic zone on the 21st, you have every right to demand lights, camera and action, and if he didn't and can't supply it now, he should be ditched for someone who can. On the 24th, Saturn provides you with the sound initiative to realize that anyone who doesn't have your best interests at heart is not good enough. And around the emotional Full Moon of the 26th, you have the confidence to head into the New Year with a man worthy of your affections. Share them generously for blissfully festive sexual fun under the mistletoe and beyond.

Your Love
Horoscope
2004

Libra
The Scales

September 23 – October 22

Love Check

Why you're fabulous

- Charming the pants off him is your favourite pastime.
- You always look serene, glamorous and alluring.
- Romantic and idealistic, you always make your relationship a harmonious place to be.

Why you're impossible

- You flirt at parties just to keep him on his toes.
- Being nice all the time means he never knows how you really feel.

Your love secrets

- If you're not in a relationship you'll find your way into someone's heart with the greatest of ease.
- Some men just can't live up to your high expectations and then you feel letdown.
- You always look at life in terms of 'we' and assume every man you meet does too.

Your sexual style

Classy, passive and aesthetically beautiful.

Who falls for you

All types, because they see in you an image of feminine perfection. Streetwise hunks who adore your rational outlook on life and strong earthy types who want to bring out the wild woman in you.

Who you fall for

Independent tearaways, whizz kids with time and money to devote to you, fiery men with a dare factor or intellectual cool customers, as long as they are all beautiful.

You identify with

Love triangles, perfect manners and beauty and truth. Designers, glamorous celebrities and men who know the difference between Manet and Monet.

Your greatest temptation

Imagining there's someone better round the next corner.

Your greatest strength

Knowing that love really does make the world go round.

Passion Profile for 2004

The year starts on a sexual high note with Mars jet-setting through your relationship zone, boosting your ego and libido just when you need it. But your deep desire for a close relationship might get in the way of a good time by scaring off one potential partner. This is just one of those years when you are hungry for love. The seductive influence of your ruler Venus throughout the spring forces the issue to break, bringing dazzling realization of a mismatch between your ego and your ideals. When Venus backtracks through your chart through May and June, it feels as if someone is holding up a mirror to your past. You're learning a lot from how things were and now you know what it is that's most important to your life. And that's to appreciate those you love most, including yourself, now your values are changing dramatically and for the better. Your new outlook encourages flirtatious fun and romance aplenty in July. And by the end of November you embark on an incredible romantic adventure. Whether it's a physical, intellectual or emotional journey, you're stunningly optimistic and you have every reason to be. Your destiny will be everything you want it to be and more. And now that you've learned to love yourself, so can someone else.

2004 Month by Month

January

With Mars's feisty influence in Aries this month, you're in the mood for stealing the show and for proving how seductive you can be without even smiling your most enigmatic smile. When it matters, your Libran charm won't let you down and you'll feel vitalized and delicious, sophisticated and oozing with feminine charm. Stow away that 'dream-catcher', because this is a month for turning your dreams into reality.

The Full Moon on the 7th gives a boost to your income and increases your desire to spend. A brief temptation to splash out on something you don't really need makes you reconsider whether pleasing others all the time is actually giving you a true sense of self-worth. Isn't it odd how when you actually please yourself and stick to your own rules you don't get caught up in making compromises and having to mould your time and effort around one boyfriend's needs or problems?

A lack of communication with your lover mid-month makes you feel restless and uneasy – usually you'd walk out of the door or depart promptly to avoid any scenes, but just this once it's worth sticking out the discomfort. Talk things over with him on the 15th, shower him with the affection he craves and he'll repay you in the only way he knows how. And by the 26th you'll truly know that your heart is in the right place.

For the last few months you've been feeling relaxed and you've enjoyed the lively social life you've created both out and about and at home. As Venus cruises through Pisces from the 15th, the chill January winds give way to a steamy rapport with someone special. You're both in the mood for spontaneous sexual fun, whether at home or in secret public places, just to see how much you can get away with. Accept those invites this month and don't think twice about what to wear – you're at your most irresistible, so make those quick intuitive flashes about where to go and how to dress and you'll exude a warmth and passion for life wherever you go.

While Neptune and Uranus are gliding gently forward, the unpredictable and often elusive behaviour of a new boyfriend or romantic fling suddenly seems less confusing. Unusual or highly creative people will still come and go in your social and romantic life, but you'll feel creative, passionate and flattered by the attention. Your sense of humour will be desirable, and if you're looking for romance and chance encounters, you'll be able to seduce anyone who catches your eye. Watch out on the 29th if you're single, a seductive rogue has his eyes on you.

February

Domestic urges take hold from the 1st, but dinner *a deux* can be a bit heavy, so arrange a picnic with a difference to get his juices flowing. Novelty is everything and you're fabulously inventive, especially around the 4th. Invite your current lover to dine in a deserted field or riverbank and forget the plates. It might be a chilly February, but with Valentine's day giving you all kinds of fantastic ideas for sexy fun, anywhere that is different, daring or spontaneous will give you both a superb sexual rapport.

Venus moves on into Aries on the 9th, while Mars challengingly moves on through sensual Taurus. There seems to be a feeling that someone's sending out mixed messages, but if they're playing with your emotions, could it be that you're reading the signals wrong?

Around the 20th, the New Moon brings you an urge to go out on a professional limb. And an upswing in your ambitious drive could bring a seriously sexy admirer out of the filing cabinet who was too nervous to approach you before. By the 27th, your seductive wiles are so finely honed that he won't be able to resist. (If you're already attached, then it might just be the test to see how deeply involved you really are.) Flirt gently, touch his arm and hold his gaze, and he'll be desperate to get beneath those layers and under your duvet. Let him peel you naked like an onion and the only tears before bedtime will be those of ecstatic bliss.

March

The Full Moon on the 6th fuels you with fantastic ideas to fulfil your potential and find new ways to express yourself. Joining an evening class could bring the satisfaction you desire. Indulge yourself in writing, painting, clay modelling or music. It's here you're most likely to meet a sexy soulmate. Whether he's a fellow student or posing naked as a model, he's probably interested in more than just your artistic talent. Venus is pulling you towards all the gorgeous things life has to offer, be it a romantic romeo or a new pair of boots. The superficial might be just what you fancy, but is it what you need? There's only one way to find out. Indulge yourself in pure bodily pleasures and by the 18th you could end up playing a duet you're so in tune with one another.

With the Aries New Moon on the 20th you're feeling even more inventive and Mercury gives you the voice to express your sexual desires. Venus's seductive allure in sexy Taurus means you just can't go wrong where your sensual fulfilment is concerned. But take care at the end of the month when your thoughts turn to work. It's not that you want to cut ties or break up a good thing when it's staring you in the face, but you begin to notice that your integrity and directness are being admired by a person in a key position. Just don't let too much heady ambition cloud the importance of one special and very sensual relationship. You might want to go out and lunch, flirt and have the chance of a promotional break, but make sure you keep your mobile switched on – there's a chance that special person might just call you and remind you that love is a very precious thing.

April

The Full Moon in your own sign on the 5th gives a boost to your personal self-esteem. You'll feel in the mood for love, so enjoy the devotion and attention you're about to receive. If you're feeling worried about your relationship and the major changes that are occurring in your life, then make sure on the 20th you express your thoughts to your lover. Sexually, this a time of deep understanding between you and him, but it could feel as if everything you say and do just doesn't seem to ring true. By the 29th, you'll have worked out any difficulties and your energy levels will be at their peak, so enjoy the physical bliss. If you're single, look out on the 14th for a dreamy type who lingers around you like a honeybee. He could be younger than you so enjoy the attention, and if you're ready for romance, keep your eyes fixed firmly on him.

An ex seems confused around the 22nd, so stay your most unruffled and poised. What matters this month is your inner peace, not other people's chaos. You know you still care about him, but he might be expecting you to fall into the same kind of codependent relationship that you know isn't right for you.

The New Moon on the 19th makes you feel decidedly passionate and full of 'oomph'. Your sexual energy levels will be on a high, so take advantage of this vitality, and if you're attached, a mixture of friendly affection and sexual pleasure will do wonders for your ego.

With Venus and Mars dancing through your adventurous zone, take the chance to explore new ideas, goals and even that sneaky little word 'commitment' with a boyfriend. Rarely do you admit to your own deeper emotions, simply because you feel more at ease about being rational and reasonable. But you could experience a moment of anxiety about being desperate and needy on the 26th, simply because sometimes you have to admit to having feelings. If your lover understands that your sparkle, wit and charm are also an expression of your deeper desire for harmony, then he'll be closer to you than ever before. Show him you care, give him the support and attention he craves at the moment and you'll be rewarded with a genuinely deeper and more satisfying relationship.

If you're single, flash your sexiest smile at that optimist with a twinkle in his eye on the 29th – he's either in the same building, dealing on the stock exchange or hanging out in the most expensive restaurants. When you meet him you're up for a seriously idyllic liaison.

May

You are an idealist so don't expect your lover or boyfriend to live up to your vision of how love should be. Love is a mental process for you; of course it involves your feelings but you view it through the romancing ideals of your mind rather than living it through the experience of your other senses. You do have a heart, but it is governed by your mind. While your ruler Venus is retrograde from the 17th onwards this month, come down from your brain and rediscover your heart. When you seek it out, and if you discover that love is about good old reality as well as the images and romantic notions that you treasure, then true love won't be so illusory or disappointing after all.

If you're looking for harmony, which you usually are, don't be afraid to air your thoughts on the 13th and show how utterly magical and warm-hearted you can be to those who matter. The 22nd is a day when you could feel as if all your dreams will come true. The next moment you could feel totally vulnerable because your romantic dreams just seem confusing and totally unrealistic. Illusions are wonderful until they become disillusions, but if you accept that with disillusionment comes awareness and acceptance of reality, then you can begin to brew your own love potions based on knowing who you are rather than what you think others might expect from you. Don't compromise this month, just stay aware of your limitations as well as your charm and charisma, and you'll discover that love isn't an illusion unless you choose to let it be so.

June

Jupiter's influence makes partying and having fun top priority from the 2nd, and your ruler Venus's provocative influence has you writing limericks and spinning tales to laugh an especially sexy lover into your arms and onto the bed. Use Mercury's entertaining charms to take the seduction one step further.

Tangling yourself up in a self-made web of intrigue is all too easy around the 17th when Venus squares up to Jupiter and temporarily blocks lines of communication. If he hasn't called or e-mailed, don't leap to conclusions – consider all the options before jumping down his throat. At least wait a couple of days or your reaction might make him think you're too keen. Hang out with friends, enjoy drinking and smooching in the sun, and you'll come to realize you're so in demand you needn't worry. When Mars moves into Leo on the 24th, you'll recognize your chance for real happiness and how to obtain it. Dazzling self-belief and certainty of where you're heading is irresistible and sees you rising from the ashes with one very sexy *amour* clinging to your feathers.

July

Romantic dreams fill your days and the summer brings new flirtations and a run of exciting days throughout the month, whether at home or on holiday. At last you can feel confident about your most personal of objectives and trust your own judgement without fearing the disapproval of others. Things have been so up in the air concerning your home and family ties recently, but now you can come to terms with making the necessary changes, even if they are not exactly according to your true desires. Confusion surrounding your thoughts about your inner security and sense of stability have made you moody lately, but now everything's changing and you'll feel vibrant, alive and ready to take on the world.

With so much planetary activity in the area of your chart concerning relaxation and a sense of wellbeing this month, you'll also be happy to take a break from the fray to enjoy a cosy night in or a relaxing night out with friends around the New Moon on the 17th. This is an important time for you to exchange information with your pals about your personal happiness and how you need to develop certain aspects of your life, both financially and materially, to acquire the level and standard of lifestyle that you truly need. There's plenty of opportunity to make yourself heard around the 24th, when Venus opposes Pluto, and money, possessions and inner values need to be sorted out with your partner. So listen to what he has to say first, then make any shrewd changes according to your own beliefs. For once don't compromise for the sake of argument; you need to stick to your principles, however easier it would be to give in.

August

With Mars sneaking into the area of your chart concerning secrets, seclusion and dreams on the 8th, this month looks set to be the beginning of a new phase if you're single, as you could be about to embark on a new and breathtaking love affair. However, it will be discreet and secretive – a clandestine romance or an affair with a man who lives in a dream world. Whatever the scenario, when you bump into him in your social whirl you'll know this is a deeply mysterious relationship, whatever the outcome. Charismatic and enchanting, Venus gives you the seductive powers of Cleopatra, and even though you begin to worry there's a rival in your social circle who's after the same man, get out and be the life and soul of the party. Around the 15th, your personal charm and self-confident approach to love and life gets you noticed, desired and hunted by that gorgeous enigmatic admirer.

If you're already attached, August marks an emotional turning point. You start to open up about your needs and how it's essential to keep alive the romance and passion in your relationship. Also, don't forget that although you need to feel part of a double act, you must also honour your own individuality. That means finding the space to develop your career or ambitions, and still having time for friends as well. Tell your boyfriend honestly how you feel around the Full Moon on the 30th, and if you are true to your own vision, you can begin to create the kind of relationship that really works for you.

September

Commitment in a love relationship is really what you're searching for and if you feel you aren't getting as much back as you give out you can resort to sudden and surprising measures. And forcing a lover to make an all-or-nothing decision means you might end up lonely. Yet with the calming effects of Venus, you begin to accept that reflection and adjustment are necessary rather than leaping in at the deep end.

With Saturn forcing you to make compromises, you feel like you're taking one step forward and then ending up two steps back. Don't worry, this means that however insecure you feel about your relationship, there is a purpose behind the impasse. Around the 15th, he seems to be holding back on his feelings, but with your extraordinary insight you'll know you were right about his underlying motives, so speak up and reveal your unspoken desires. Now is the time to put your intuition to the test and show him that your secretive and sometimes intensely powerful feelings are only reserved for the best possible man in your life.

If you're single, you have an uncanny feeling that somehow that ultimate relationship is about to kick-start. And with Jupiter and Mars moving into your own sign on the 25th, followed by a stunning link up on the 26th, watch out for fireworks of the most wicked kind. Even if you're attached you might find yourself attracted to someone who you'd never normally have noticed.

A mature business associate or a streetwise player could be worth your hypnotic gaze – if not for love then always for fun. You're at your most delectable and magnetic, so don't miss those opportunities to show off your extraordinary charisma. Don't worry if you feel guilty about accepting an invite around the 28th when you think you should be juggling with deadlines, the feeling will definitely pass. Seize the chance to take a long overdue break and enjoy friends, lovers and, most of all, yourself.

This is a month when the most important thing to remember is that understanding and acknowledging your feelings reveals not only what you truly want from a relationship but also deep down inside what your greatest desires are. More than at any other time of the year, now is your chance to really focus on your love goals and ambitions for the future, and to know that whatever conclusion you reach will always be the right one.

October

A super month for pleasures of the flesh as well as of the mind. The 1st is a brilliant day when you can be at your most charismatic and passionate where one lover is concerned. Make sure you assert your sexual desires if you're planning a night in with him. By the Solar eclipse in your own sign on the 14th you'll be indulging in sexual intimacy at home. If not, you'll feel in the mood for erotic conversation, so switch that mobile phone on. Expect an unusual invite for a wicked adventure on the 19th. He's got it into his head he has to keep up with your libido. And, actually, he's right for once.

A fascinating and unusual romantic encounter occurs on the 21st, just when you expected to spend a few days alone. By the next day you'll be at your most stunning and sexually buzzing, so if you're after his phone number make sure you memorize it before he does a disappearing act. Venus surges on into your own sign around the 29th and, if you're single, you'll feel a sudden surge of adrenalin and start craving a gorgeous male colleague. Take advantage of the energy to let him know you're drooling. What matters most this month is your own desire and satisfaction. You just can't give up now on all those dreams and romantic desires, now that you are about to discover a new and deeply moving experience – in more ways than one.

This is an excellent month for communicating your sexual needs without getting into a tangle of interests. If you're breathlessly waiting for an e-mail or phone call from your man, then your vibrant personality won't let him forget you. Your boyfriend could get too possessive around the 17th when you'd rather be dreaming of an escape route. By the 28th you'll have realized why sometimes that twosome thing you need so much is important to you, but you also have to have a personal sense of liberty, financial control and social contacts. It's time to set the record straight. Sexual passion, yes, commitment to the washing-up bowl, never!

November

Life is pulling you in more directions than you've ever been pulled before, but as a Libran, isn't that just how you like it? Sadly, it's not a string of sexy studs fighting over your body, but a battle for time between work, home life and relationships. Luckily, the celestial influence brings serious love action to your workplace, so even when you're involved with professional conundrums you can get up to some extracurricular activities.

With Mars moving on into sexy Scorpio on the 11th, you're blessed with extra special charms and can express your sensual beauty. Your imagination and perception are pin sharp on the 5th, so be sure to use them to check out who's doing what to whom. There's a secret rival out there, and even if you're sure your relationship is absolutely rock solid or that one love interest only has eyes for you, just take care when making any last-minute arrangements so you don't get caught up in a very embarrassing mistake. But around the 29th, thanks to Jupiter's deceptive liaison with Neptune, you might play one too many games yourself or find you've shared your secrets with too many friends, but at least any romantic panics have calmed down to a slightly less frenetic pace and you know where you stand. So take a few quiet moments to put an end to a secret flirtation or affair that's run its course. You'll feel so much better for it that you might be tempted to take up a sexy away-day offer with a new admirer who has integrity, belief and the ability to treat you as a real equal. This is one of those romantic adventures that boosts your ego, arouses your libido but, most of all, makes you feel good to be you.

December

Creative thoughts and urges are bubbling over and you know something needs to be done, but you're not sure what. Neither are you in the mood to ask awkward questions, until the New Moon on the 12th, when your eyes are suddenly opened wide and you're given a clear vision of what you have to do to make an important relationship work. Mars and Venus propel you to throw out long-held ideas and ideals for a wonderfully fresh approach. By the 16th, you know what you want for Christmas and it's more than just a stocking filler. A wonderful surge of strength allows you to share your desires and ask the question you've been avoiding. Does he love you or is it just lust? The truth brings things to a head, and by the time of the Full Moon in Cancer on the 26th, you'll either be well on your way to coupledom or surrounded by sexy hunks on a mission to snag a hot date, thanks to your glamorous new image.

Now the question is, does Santa know if you've been naughty or nice? Even if he doesn't, the one man that matters does know and he's beginning to understand that you don't need tinsel and mistletoe to prove you're loved, you just need the joy of being together. So give him the biggest treat of all – your gorgeous self, slowly unwrapped and eagerly awaiting the kind of sexy delights that will see you through the festive frivolities. What happens next? It's a secret. But just to give you an inkling: any wishes made on New Year's Eve are very likely to come true.

Your Love
Horoscope
2004

Scorpio
The Scorpion

October 23 – November 22

Love Check

Why you're fabulous

 Erotic and mysterious, you can sexually inspire any man you want.

 You are passionate about life and love, so it's all or nothing when it comes to relationships and work.

 Friends know they can trust you with their secrets. Rivals know not to cross your path.

Why you're impossible

 You can become totally obsessed with sex.

 When you want someone or something your tactics are very manipulative.

Your love secrets

 Taking control of sexual relationships is a way of defending your vulnerability.

 You are intensely probing but give little away about yourself.

 Sex must be a transformative experience.

Your sexual style

Hypnotic, intense and totally, all-consumingly passionate.

Who falls for you

Serious men who want to transform your life forever, sensual rogues and gypsy types, men with secrets, money or another partner hidden away somewhere.

Who you fall for

Artistic types, style gurus, practical down-to-earth hunks with money in their wallet, rock stars or men who are already involved with someone else.

You identify with

Mystery, magic and intrigue. Survivors, people who are dark horses and anyone who can talk about sex, money and death.

Your greatest temptation

Men with money or power.

Your greatest strength

You will never submit to anyone or anything.

Your Love
Horoscope
2004

Passion Profile for 2004

At the beginning of the year you have to decide between bagging a personal goal or maintaining a happy-clappy relationship, and your need for challenge probably wins this January. Flirty February is sensuous, with Mars stimulating your desires and causing all sorts of delicious trouble. In early March, a domestic reorganization causes emotional upheaval and battles with a loved one, spurred on by disruptive Uranus and deceptive Neptune, and you reach a major turning point from which there is no return. Spring starts with a scorcher, as the Sun moves into your relationships zone on May 9. You suddenly discover that you can have your cake and eat it. As Jupiter enters the free-spirited and ambitious area of your chart come September, the message is to go for gold. Aspire to your wildest dreams and MAKE them come true. Idealistic Jupiter blurs those realistic romantic expectations, but you'll be approaching 2005 like a rocket launcher, indulging every whim and dream head-on. The results will be like the best firework display you ever saw. Go light those touch-papers!

2004 Month by Month

January

One professional goal is in sight this month, thanks to Jupiter's influence, and you feel quite driven to pursue success. You know that your sense of achievement ranks above all else and you're up for a challenge, but, frankly, the kind of love experiences that infiltrate your life this month will keep you doubly busy and provide just as much excitement as your working ambitions.

You know how you adore living undercover? Well, this is your month for discretion, tact and secrecy. On the 15th, Venus moves into the area of your chart concerning romantic encounters and, above all else, mystery. So for most of January, be prepared for feeling ultra mysterious, because your hypnotic aura will seriously give you the chance of meeting someone who could prove to be a secret fling or, at the very least, someone who is intriguing and magnetic. Alternatively, if you're involved in difficult dealings at work, this could be an important mysterious contact who puts you in the picture and clears up all those nagging fears and doubts you have about someone you haven't felt ready to trust. You'll have to be ultra cautious about expressing your personal views to those who don't really count in your life. Wait until the 21st before revealing any deeper truths, when any feelings of self-doubt which crept up on you on the 5th begin to disappear.

If you're attached and have been feeling just a teeny bit left out in the cold recently, a sudden surge of affection and devotion around the 15th from your partner makes you feel passionate and intensely sexy. Your enigmatic and sophisticated image is there to attract and allure and you'll be in the mood for a total seduction number. Even if he doesn't respond by offering to take you to the Moon and back, it might just be that deep down he's worried about where your relationship is going. Do you want total commitment, and does he? You know that creative transformation in your relationships is important, otherwise you stagnate. So make sure that all your cards are on the table and you speak up about those things which truly matter to you.

February

You're at your most smouldering this month, so use your incredible talent for getting to the heart of any matter and clarify your lover's true intentions on the 9th. The likelihood is he's confused about his role in your relationship or can't see where he fits into your amazing independent lifestyle. Do you have space for him in your life, and if you are ready to share more of it with him, is there something missing or inhibited about your personal life together? With Mars crashing headlong into your relationship zone on the 3rd, you won't have time to be analytical about your emotions – you'll be feeling ready to air your views, so be as emotionally honest as you dare.

The Full Moon on the 6th promises a night of sexual bliss with your lover, and if you're single, a spellbinding encounter raises your adrenalin levels to a delicious peak. If you stay poised and secretive, you know you'll hypnotize him with your magnetic aura. Intimate pleasure is guaranteed and you'll radiate a fabulous aura of feminine sexuality and magical mystery. Just take care around the New Moon on the 20th – you may be thinking eternal bliss, he may be more confrontational than you thought. It's not that you're doing anything wrong, just that those unspoken feelings between you are making him a little uncomfortable so try to understand that he might also fear your intense and powerfully controlling nature. As much as you feel love, you can feel hate – they aren't mutually exclusive.

March

When you are at your most profound you are usually trying to resolve a deep problem or get to the bottom of a mystery in someone else's life. This month you need to analyze and probe the depths of your own feelings, when the cosmos forces you to confront a growing sense of restlessness. Unpredictable Uranus triggers off your desire for some kind of domestic reorganization around the 10th. With professional changes in the wind and a sense of a better lifestyle ahead, it feels as if you need to move on. But a lover is ultra-suspicious of your motives and you just can't seem to say the right thing. Every time you try to explain that you're tired of the place where you live or it's time to improve your domestic set-up, he becomes less and less responsive. Don't forget that he might be feeling insecure and imagining you're about to split up. However, it's more likely that because you're getting on with living your life to the full and your self-esteem is growing daily, he's feeling a little left out in the cold.

With Venus and Mars in your relationship zone until the 21st, you panic about his distance one day and the next wonder why you had any doubts about his commitment to you. Clarity about the roles you both play and your involvement with one another will be easily understood. You'll be at your most demanding and in the mood to expose some seriously strong feelings by the 26th. And you finally reach a mutual acceptance of what you both want for the future. The powerful presence of your charisma is totally haunting, so take the opportunity to make a more serious commitment if you're sure of your own feelings.

Whether single or attached, a dazzling knight in shining armour could come into your life. Watch out for that lingering look on the stairs or in the lift, or even after office hours in the local meeting place. This is someone who will perhaps notice you before you notice him. I must admit this is pretty unusual for a Scorpio because usually you see everything that goes on around you before anyone else. Your perception is as powerful as an eagle, but this time someone's beaten you to it. Be prepared for an adventure of a lifetime to begin if you're single. If you're attached, well, isn't it nice to be desired and wanted?

April

The changes you are experiencing emotionally regarding your roots and family are important because they are giving you a sense of your own set of values, yet since the beginning of the year you have been caught up in deceit, disruption and confusion about where, and with whom, your loyalties really lie. Now you begin to feel the pressure lift and you're ready to honour your own emotional needs.

Passion is Scorpio's watchword and if you have a boyfriend or lover, then intimate moments will turn to larger than life experiences on the 23rd and 24th. With the Sun in Taurus from the 20th, your own powers of persuasion and hypnotic charm are enhanced, so get your powerful magnetic radiance in shape and be ready for a total seduction number. Tip: Bathe in candlelight and imagine him with you. If you're single, an outrageous invite on the workfront will lead to a close encounter of the sexy kind, so keep yourself 'purrfectly' lovely and mysterious while there's social whirls or office political partying going on.

Get-togethers among friends and shared experiences will take up most of your social life this month, as Mercury's backtracking effects through your relationship zone from the 5th to the 30th puts a hold on deeper romantic commitments. But as a Water-born sign, you know you need close intimate friends and are wary of those you can't trust. This month, however, you will become fascinated with new and unfamiliar acquaintances who will prove to be of value in your current quest for self-discovery. Your intuition is spot on so you'll instantly smell out any rats, users or time-wasters.

Your powerful sexual energy will be radiating in all the right directions after the 15th and sensual needs and even sexual fantasies will become a reality. So keep the latter positive and very legal. Indulge in your dreams, but remember you may have to pay the price for double-dating. Frankly, a whirlwind affair may be irresistible, but you could lose another lover in the process.

May

Pursuing not only your dreams and future plans this month but generally pursuing relationship experiences will become a high priority, as the Sun remains in your relationship zone until the 21st. You are in demand and loving it, so be at your most passionate and live by your principles and your visions. Sometimes the romantic light dims but rarely does it become clouded by doubts for very long. Your natural optimism and joy of living will give you more reason to listen to yourself than anyone else this month.

With a Full Moon in your own sign on the 4th and the New Moon in your intimate zone on the 19th, this is a month to remind yourself that transformation comes from within as well as from without. And because you've been very secretive about your feelings, be ready for an unexpected outburst from an ex-lover or a new *amour* who wants to know why you're being so mysterious. Now is your chance to reveal your own motives and how radical you can be when it comes to expressing what it is you truly want for the future. But take care on the 28th when you could be tactless without realizing it. Sometimes you say little but your partner knows exactly how you feel, sometimes you say a lot and he doesn't know where on earth he stands. This is a real test to find the balance and show that you're not holding anything back nor projecting your fears or doubts onto him – and then at least you're giving each other the chance to see if you have different needs and desires that you both assume you have. So rational communication with him is essential this month. It's time to take some kind of responsibility for your mutual aims and ambitions. Speak with conviction and honesty and you'll be amazed how logic and reason can turn the tables exactly the way you want them to be.

June

If you're attached, deceitful moments abound on the 8th and 9th, so be careful to put your heart where your mouth is. Really mean what you say to a boyfriend – he could be assuming that serious physical involvement means forever. Tell him you care, but you're a free-range bird not a battery chicken. By the 26th he'll be realizing how sexually dynamic you are. Take the lead but do so gently. He's not used to the fact that you need to be in control. Sexual domination is an art, so play it for all you can and he'll be in heaven. This could of course mean that you're always going to be in control of the affair, but doesn't that give you the intense kind of sexual pleasure you truly desire?

Enjoy an erotic encounter on the 29th when you bump into the kind of man you'd be happy to wash his socks for. The chemistry makes you feel sexy and charismatic. Resist the temptation to phone him – it will keep him guessing. And if you've already fallen into a fling with a gorgeous rogue then you won't even worry about the phone calls – just wait for the champagne on ice and your heart will instantly melt.

But if you're single and lonely, thinking about romance isn't necessarily going to help you find it this month – you have to make an effort to go out and be seen. So if you're after a quick fling, then choose your holiday spot with care. You need adventure and excitement and the kind of men who thrive on dynamic action. Plan your break around the 8th and you'll be spoilt for choice – both for men and destinations. Romance is in the air from the 13th, and on the 17th an idealistic rebel turns you on momentarily, but then you have to run like hell when you realize he's ultra serious about universal love. You would prefer that his passion was all for you. After all, do you really want to share his body with anyone else?

July

This month could be the most sexy and spicy one ever if you're happy to wait patiently for that phone call from your man. But perhaps the more intelligent thing to do is to get on with your social life and keep him guessing. Once he realizes you have a life of your own you can begin to assert your sexual needs. Be careful on the 5th, if you become too possessive he might put the brakes on commitment. By the 9th, you'll be dazzling and feeling raunchy enough to forget your differences. It will be worth it. After the 20th, it's time to get those personal issues resolved. New sexual techniques are on your mind on the 30th, so make sure you give him a guiding hand before you attempt the unimaginable.

You'll be looking your most sensual and luscious this month, so if you're feeling left out in the cold then don't worry, there's someone out there who's taken notice. Watch out on the 14th for an eccentric untamed rogue and on the 15th for a charmer with a twinkle in his eye. You are certainly ready to have a light-hearted affair, but anything that is more compromising and intense could be short-lived and painful. Avoid getting too involved, too soon, however much you think this is the man for you.

You're wondering how, where and who is doing what to whom among your friends and their tangled intrigues. Whatever you do, keep your usual sensible head and play it cool around the 17th. A platonic contact and a good friend of your favourite pal is beginning to want more than just a chat.

The Venus-Pluto opposition on the 24th sends shudders of desire through your nerve endings. Tell your man what your sexual needs are and you'll be wickedly rewarded. Sexually you have nothing to prove, but it's time to show that you have all kinds of different sensual desires. Suggest you share champagne and strawberries al fresco on a balmy night around the 29th. What you do with the fruit is entirely up to you. Orgasmically you're both in tune, but if you feel he still doesn't understand you, speak openly about what actually turns you wild. You'll be in sexy heaven.

August

Mars surges into the high-flying corner of your chart and your ambition knows no bounds. It's not just professional success on the agenda, you've probably got your eye on a rather tasty personal ambition too. A Mars-Pluto square on the 6th gives you the confidence and drive to pursue all your goals. Demand a promotion and at the same time pin that hunk down to a time and place. Your libido is raging, so make the place here and the time NOW! Nothing other than sexual passion will satisfy nature's urges, so like a Boy Scout, be prepared. As Venus moves into your dream zone on the 7th, you'll be rerunning clips of the night's action. Meanwhile, the Sun's relationship to Pluto allows for a second bite of the cherry – and this time it's blissfully sensual, not just sexual.

While Mercury turns turtle until the 25th, you're unsure about whether to get sexually involved with someone who could put you in a position of power. Talk things through with a confidential and impartial friend. And not until you're 100 per cent convinced should you commit yourself verbally either way. Other than your mother, no-one has your best interests at heart, so don't believe otherwise.

The New Moon on the 16th ends a domestic problem and by the end of the month you rediscover a treasured possession you lost at a party. Whether it's of physical or sentimental value, you'll be glad that it's found its way back. Or do I mean, you'll be glad that *he's* found his way back?

September

Play the field and flatter, but don't lose sight of reality, as the Sun, Mars and Jupiter rush on through the idealistic and ambitious area of your chart this month. It's time to maintain your individuality and go after what you truly want in life. Don't feel you're letting anyone down, because the one person who matters this month is you. Oh, and by the way, throwing yourself into arranging a major social event around the 10th is a much safer bet than throwing yourself into the arms of a sexy rogue who wants to lead you astray.

You shouldn't believe all you hear this month, as Neptune's influence makes everything and everyone seem attractive. Your instincts are not as reliable as usual, so work hard and lie low. Avoid doing anything which could damage your reputation around the 17th, but use your head and not your heart to throw yourself into a bigger and better cause.

It's hard to fend off unwanted attention from the 18th, with Venus's seductive influence bringing you oodles of glamour and charisma, but stick by those people, events and professional contacts you know and trust. Around the 26th, Mars and Jupiter's passionate alliance triggers off a desire for someone who is already attached. You just can't stop thinking about them and your craving for them reaches obsessional proportions. If you follow up on your temptation, take care you don't get found out. With Venus's help you're irresistible, so why resist? By the end of the month you realize that he's not so besotted as you thought, but at least you've had the kind of passionate encounter you'll remember for a long time.

October

Nostalgic memories are enough to make you blush this month, when you realize and mentally replay the greatest sex you ever had – with an ex-lover. Around the Solar eclipse of the 14th, you're considering doing something about it. Either establish contact with that gorgeous ex- or recreate the sexual fantasies you shared with your current lover and October will be hotter than July. Show him what you want and find sensations or words that stimulate you both. You're still likely to be stuck in an emotional rut around the 10th, but Mercury swoops into your own sign and you realize it's time to communicate your deepest emotional needs.

It's hard not to drift from relationship to dissatisfactory relationship, as Neptune keeps you wondering what is real and what is an illusion until the 24th, but there's light at the end of the tunnel. Come the 27th, you're blessed with the intellectual capacity to manoeuvre yourself into a situation which is truly best for you and could involve starting afresh. The total eclipse of the Moon on the 28th fires up your imagination and you feel much stronger. By the 31st, you meet someone who has the same sexual appetites and desires as you. Suddenly what's present completely overshadows what's past in every way imaginable – but more than ever in the boudoir.

November

You surge into your birthday month with a vengeance, accepting dates, organizing parties and playing Miss Congeniality. The New Moon of the 12th gives you a chance to do a nifty about-turn, changing the direction you've been moving in, to live life to the cut of your own cloth. We're talking gold-embroidered silk here. The planetary activity in your chart makes you imaginative, optimistic and artistic, attracting well-heeled, sexy rogues to cater to your every whim. Be at your most magical and wicked as you enjoy the sensuous pleasures of being wined and dined, and your admirer will beg to see you again. But don't trust anyone with your secrets around the 11th, when Mars hustles into Scorpio and lessens your usual clear judgement and intuition. Some things are best left unsaid, however deep the urge is to clear your conscience.

Surprise a special hunk on the 22nd by showing him the power of your physical strength and your seductive beauty. Venus subtly moves into your own sign too, so you're in the mood to take control and you could be more persistent than ever before. You know that you have to stay on top of your feelings, but just this once you can't resist being more carefree and wild than you've been for a long time. Enjoy the thrills of dressing up, put on something danger-ously sexy, spin Madonna's 'Erotica' and take him in hand. Have it all your way and by the 27th you might be in the mood to consider a return match – and this time, let him take control.

December

With Mars and Venus still in your own sign until nearly Christ-mas, you have enough charisma to seduce a football team, but you know better uses for it. Your financial ability is finely honed and you're in the mood to strike a bargain and clinch a deal, using any method available. By the end of the month your powers of per-suasion pays off. You've convinced a VIP contact that you're next in line for a top-notch position. Mercury's backtracking effects until the 20th gives you time to consider your moves, but use it to con-sider some festive action too. Implement that Venusian charisma to seduce a colleague into giving you an up-close-and-personal Christmas present. A dreamy hunk is your passport to happiness so put on your party glitter and flirt your way past any so-called rivals.

Watch out around the 15th, someone's out to manipulate you and make you keen by playing the jealousy card – and it works. But if they have to make you green to get you interested, the rela-tionship lacks natural sparkle, so think twice. Around the 18th, you're aroused to start something new with the help of passionate Pluto – this time, make sure your man deserves delectable you. By the 25th, you're as popular as chocolate. Take the sentiment of goodwill to all men seriously and enjoy blazing a trail of sensual excitement into the New Year. And that's just the beginning, there's more to come. And one relationship which may have been foundering now looks set for a complete revamp or transformation, on your terms.

Your Love
Horoscope
2004

Sagittarius

The Archer

November 23 – December 20

Your Love
Horoscope
2004

Love Check

Why you're fabulous

 You inspire friends and lovers by being an eternal optimist.

You are utterly romantic and always enticing.

Why you're impossible

You rarely relax and restlessly search for new experiences.

You can deliver verbal punches without thinking if they'll hurt.

Your love secrets

For you, sex is a celebration of life.

You need personal freedom more than anything in the world and are happiest single.

Domesticity is the last thing on your mind, sex is the first!

Your sexual style

♐ Direct, passionate and highly provocative.

Who falls for you

♐ Action men, adventurous rogues, intellectuals who adore your get-up-and-go attitude to life and practical possessive types who want to tame you.

Who you fall for

♐ Independent hustlers, men who've travelled, experienced no-nonsense tycoons, celebrities and rich kids.

You identify with

♐ A fast-paced and action-packed career and love of life. The unknown or anything which challenges your mind – particularly men.

Your greatest temptation

♐ Making wild promises you know you won't keep.

Your greatest strength

♐ A hilarious approach to life and love.

Passion Profile for 2004

This year is a sexual roller coaster, taking you from sensual thrills to romantic highs, and occasionally plummeting into depths of guilt. Early on in the year you're hampered by your own impatience and it's clear that respect for your individual needs isn't something you're willing to give up. Spring adds a guilty secret to your problems, thanks to your ruler Mars wreaking havoc between your heart and your loins, and an overseas influence has a major impact on your plans. But Venus's U-turn in your relationship zone from May 17 to June 29 encourages a more enlightened outlook and rational recognition of your emotional dreams. No longer seeking escape, you face up to your feelings and learn about your needs and desires. You used to envy one ex-lover's independent lifestyle, but now you realize you need that kind of freedom too. July sees the return of the dashingly, racy you, but this time in hot pursuit of a relationship which is both serious and sensuous. All year round the planets highlight your ambitions and ideals, forcing an important decision. To achieve your dream you may have to end an imperfect relationship. But it's a small price to pay and soon you'll realize that you're willing to forsake something you once thought far more precious, in the name of love.

2004 Month by Month

January

You're feeling in the mood for high adventure this month, and the dance of Venus through your deeply private zone from the 15th makes you more than usually intuitive about an unbelievable but important message from a friend. Listen carefully, ignore the over-all picture, read between the lines and you'll discover something to your advantage.

The slow journey of Pluto through your own sign still brings with it the need to find a new spirit of adventure, or at the very least a sense of purpose. You're always travelling, whether it's sim-ply to a friend's place or to exotic locations, or even in the mind. Trust in your feelings this month and level with yourself if you have any fears. Scrabbling around in the dark won't make for trav-elling light, but getting out the map in daylight and really focussing on where you are going – with a plan of action – will.

There seems to be no easy options concerning personal choices around the 6th, but by the end of the month your faith in your abil-ity to make romantic decisions is restored. Whatever is at stake re-garding your long-term future seems strangely to resonate with your current angst. Ensure this month you plot your strategy with conviction rather than your sometimes more carefree approach. Exaggerating the truth is always fun, but sticking to the facts is often more creative. So take those relationship chances on the 21st and you won't be disappointed.

February

The Full Moon on the 6th makes for a tempting offer from a stranger – accept and discover a fantastic breath of passionate air. If you have a boyfriend or lover, take this opportunity to let him reach an agreement with you about how both your feelings matter in any joint decisions or plans. The onus will be on him to keep to his promise; after all, you know that you can win him round to any argument, and when you're feeling so ready to be fair in love and in war, the chances are he'll prefer love.

For most of the month, and especially around Valentine's Day, Venus makes you yearn for social whirls and celebrations. Beautiful men just can't resist you, so take advantage of your spontaneous charisma.

Free-spirited though you're feeling, by the 20th one boyfriend seems more demanding than ever and wants to organize your every move. Around the 23rd, you impulsively feel like packing a bag and setting off on a weekend jaunt alone or just heading off to a social venue where no-one knows you. Adventurous living is your greatest antidote to feelings of being controlled. So, of course, when a partner tries to dominate you or considers you to be one of his possessions, you end up playing the rebel. After all, with such a fiery, spontaneous streak, you just won't be bossed around by anyone. Luckily, unusual encounters and fascinating new friends give your ego a boost, and by the 25th, the same boyfriend admits he's been a little jealous and is ready to take a more light-hearted approach to your relationship. By the end of the month, you both have equal respect for each other's autonomy.

March

Around the 12th, a sudden surge of enthusiasm for changing your plans will induce a sense of adventure into your lifestyle. Now is a time when you need trust and belief from those closest to you, and however supportive you think a lover is likely to be, you could find yourself defending your quest. You feel guilty around the 16th because you fancy someone else's boyfriend and you start worrying about ever finding true love.

Spend the month clearing up loose ends rather than scattering around new ones. This is the time of the year when focussing on how you relate to others and how you relate to yourself takes on massive proportions, so don't let your plans get dishevelled by a lack of self-belief. Now is the time to light a match to your romantic dreams and watch the adventure truly begin to flame.

Watch out for an unpredictable and provocative encounter with an exotic stranger or someone from overseas around the 20th. It's not that you're in need of any more drama in your life than you already have, but this could be the chance to show your rivals what you are truly made of.

With Mars plunging into your relationship zone on the 21st, you suddenly feel more optimistic about your future relationship direction. One chapter in your love life is over and it's time to put yourself first – how can you resist? You'll be ready by the 29th to listen to seriously important advice about one admirer's interest in you, but make sure you trust your instincts and avoid trying to find an ulterior motive behind what's being put forward to you. You're motivated and in the mood for change, so check out all the options before you make any spontaneous decisions. Confrontations are inevitable, but at least you'll know exactly where you stand.

April

The New Moon in your romantic zone on the 19th makes you feel like a chilly moonlight swim with your lover, or at the very least a crazy party with a feast of friends. This exaggerated energy also means it's time to plan a short trip. You know you can't live without travelling, so go on a wild jaunt with one of your lovers on the 23rd. You never know, you might discover the truth about one of your cheating ex-partners.

With Venus now giving you the chance to be diplomacy personified, you're ready to make a more serious commitment about dealing with your personal sexual desires. It's not that you can't make up your mind about who you really want to be with, it's more that, truthfully, you just want your freedom and no strings. Of course you're a light-hearted romantic, but are you prepared to give up your freedom for a routine relationship and too many responsibilities?

If you're still notoriously single, after the 19th you'll be eye-catching first, man-catching second. And if you have a lover, watch out for an on-the-spot ravishment when you reveal your passion for sex outdoors. You know how spontaneous you are about sex, so enjoy feeling ravishing and indulge your body in truly passionate style. Orgasms are about celebration, so be prepared for the most fiery and magical of experiences.

May

With Venus backtracking through your chart on the 17th, you're still unsure whether to be more serious about love and relationships or just give it a break. Of course you have feelings, but there is a side of you that lives and yearns for excitement, danger and the unknown. And the celestial line-up is urging you to think things through. It's one of those restless months, all desires scrambling for attention, and a host of fascinating encounters gives you a chance to sort out if there's really anyone out there who understands you. Especially as your ruler Jupiter begins to creep forward again this month and makes you feel ready to take on an exciting and wild encounter. After the 21st, the Sun triggers off a passion for sexual bliss. You'll be at your most vivacious and extrovert and ready for a wild social life.

Feelings of nostalgia are rare for you, but the last week of the month is a time when the challenges of the past few months can now be reflected upon with understanding and, most of all, self-awareness. You may be in demand, loved and desired, but is that enough? Freedom and independence are just two things which can't be sacrificed – and you know it. But somehow love just has to fit into your lifestyle. Now's your chance to discover how.

June

Watch out for a fascinating smooth talker around the Full Moon in your own sign on the 3rd. He's had his eyes on you for some time but you didn't think he was sexy, until now that is. The 17th is an opportunity to haul in a dreamy-looking man via a close friend or from around the far side of the office. Check out his intentions though before you let him know you care. If you do fall into a passionate embrace, then you're guaranteed exquisitely sensual moments of passion and pleasure around the 18th, for nights you won't forget.

On the 20th, replenish your sex drive and pamper your body, mind and spirit. You'll bounce back looking radiant enough to lure any cool and aloof man into your arms. You'll feel sexually motivated, passionate and full of 'oomph' after the 24th, when Mars moves into your adventurous zone, triggering off a series of intriguing episodes.

On the 29th, when Venus starts to move forward again, you'll suddenly feel a weight has been taken away from your emotional baggage. Finally becoming friends with an ex- or giving up on past regrets gives you the confidence to enjoy being with your current man. He's seriously ready to make a further commitment as long as you are happy to fall in with his plans. They are of the sexual kind, so discover how bold, wicked and pleasurable he is between the sheets, once you open up and tell him how you truly feel.

If you're single, you're likely to bump into a fascinating stranger in an art gallery or museum this month. So look out for a romantic intellectual on your travels. By the 29th, you'll be dancing with a wild boy or caressing a new man into a frenzy of love.

July

You are loaded with grief from a boyfriend on the 1st, when provocative moments on the phone set off deeper personal differences. By the 3rd, you're either having to admit all kinds of truths to re-establish how you both feel, or at the very least you're realizing you need to get out of the stormy relationship fast. If you want to leave before it gets too complicated, do so on the 16th. If you're happier keeping things the way they are, simply take logical steps and analyze his motives and yours. Sexually you'll be at your most provocative around the 21st, so make sure he knows it too. Don't worry, you'll be feeling your normal vibrant self by the 29th.

If you're single, you'll be feeling at your most trusting on the 3rd when out of the blue comes an unusual invite or a provocative gesture from a stranger. This is what you do enjoy, surprises of the enigmatic kind. You know secretly who you adore and it's up to you later in the month to show them you mean pleasure not business. The only trouble with your logic is actually deciding out of all the contenders which one it is that you do really desire the most.

August

At last you're firmly in control of your moods again. It hasn't been easy trying to keep any man happy, let alone yourself, but the physical aspects of your life are stunning. All you need now is to relax and not let the emotional side become a bone of contention. You're on a summer buzz and a sexual high, so persuade one lover to caress you at those very spontaneous moments when you least expect it. The 4th and the 12th are days of fascination and fear about how far you can really go with him. You are notoriously unable to make a decision. Especially when you spot a new face on the workfront around the 25th and wonder if you're about to pass out with desire.

But the creative force of the Sun and Mars can help you trap that gorgeous hunk you've been dreaming about lately. Around the 1st, send him e-mails describing your wildest fantasies and you might discover that his intentions are as deliciously dishonourable as yours. Get him into a steamy clinch around the 6th, when a juicy Mars-Pluto alignment makes you hotter than a sauna and sexually devious to boot. Make those e-mail fantasies come true and be sure he satisfies your rampant libido as well as his own. He'll be exhausted after all that action, but Mars boosts your dynamism, making you sex siren of the month. Around the 10th, you're pumped full of physical energy, oozing sensuality and in the mood to dance. A string of admirers can't resist you and Venus helps you attract a seriously cute admirer.

Be careful not to vent that fiery anger around the 25th, when Mercury swings forward again in fiery Leo, giving you a wicked tongue. Tell your lover he's in the wrong and he could just find someone else to turn him on. Keep quiet and you'll be his favourite sex toy all month.

September

Hard work and sexy underwear get you noticed, and in the office there's a colleague who breaks out into a sweat every time you smile across the desk. He's steaming hot and it's not because of the weather. He's bubbling over for you, and by the time Venus moves into Leo on the 6th, he'll probably be plying you with cocktails in some trendy new bar. Even if you fancy him big time, don't give too much too soon. Now that he's drooling over you, you can demand whatever you fancy and take control. You wonder why he hasn't called around the 14th and, of course, those old anxieties about, 'Am I good enough, too thin, too tall, too short, to slim, too fat' return to haunt you. But don't get things out of proportion and don't worry, because he's still thinking seriously sexy thoughts about you.

The Full Moon of the 28th brings an end to misplaced affections, leading you on to even more exciting sensual opportunities, creating a sizzling undercurrent of sexual intensity. You're insatiable and you almost feel as if your passions must be satisfied, even at the expense of others. Someone could get hurt, but lucky Jupiter gives you creative expression to tantalize the one man who you really know could be Mr Right. As Madonna said, 'Express Yourself'. Over and over again.

October

Watch out for a high-flyer who wants to lead you astray before the 10th. This one might just be your knight in shining armour and you want more than a one-night stand, especially around the partial Solar eclipse of the 14th. So it's one of those games which only you can play successfully. If you're already attached, then take care you don't get involved in a very confusing love triangle. It's not that you want to be led astray – not just yet anyway – but it's almost as if you have little choice. By the 20th, you're being tempted by sexier offers and your enthusiasm starts to wane, and it could just be that you need a little excitement. Yet you realize that knowing someone more intimately brings a trust that makes you willing to go further than you've ever gone before.

The Full Moon on the 28th brings you full circle. One era has ended and you're beginning a new one. And you realize that your dazzling self-control and vivid fertile imagination are what's driving you on. Yes, you are an idealist where love is concerned and there might be new adventures to be experienced, lovers to try out and fun to be had. And still, you can't make up your mind about whether to give up on your sense of freedom or just resign yourself to a lifetime of monotony. But relinquishing your space doesn't necessarily mean you have to sink into domesticity. And you're beginning to realize that a serious double act is sometimes more exciting than a string of hopeless and hapless dates.

November

Thanks to Mars your sex drive surges into action, helping you discover what really turns you on. In the first three weeks of the month you'll find out much about yourself in the process. Luckily, communicative Mercury's in your own sign from the 4th, so discuss your needs with your current lover to bring greater mutual understanding. Share your secret dreams and if he's willing to act out yours, indulge his too. Your open mind and willingness to make others happy creates sensually loving bonds. But watch out around the Full Moon on the 26th when a silly remark about commitment equalling confinement brings out the rebel in you. Take care, you don't want to undo all the hard work you've put in so far. The plus side is that it gives you huge supplies of physical strength, allowing you to juggle work, partying and oodles of passionate love-making.

After the Sun's move forward on the 22nd, you're inspired by intriguing strangers if you're single, or just inspired to experiment and enjoy the delights of a joint venture if you're attached. Whether you take a jaunt abroad or just a trip on public transport, you could find yourself causing a stir. One dark horse wants to take it further, but are you willing to give up what you already have? You're full of self-control around the 29th, but Jupiter's romantic link with Neptune brings you a few moments of wishing you were footloose and fancy-free. What is it about you this year? Probably just the fact you haven't found that total romance, that complete and utter magical land where you feel content. So don't let other people's expectations of you hold you back for one second.

December

Itchy feet and restless urges to discover exotic places and erotic soulmates has you hotfooting it out of town early this month. Your audaciously direct nature, and the influence of Mars on the 2nd, ensures a string of flirtatious encounters and passionate meetings with sexy strangers. Indulging your whims helps you escape from the pressures you've been put under in the last few months.

Dazzling connections between Venus and Mars in your own sign this month brings the sort of happiness you've only ever dreamt about. You're being appreciated by someone who makes you feel highly sensual and good about yourself. Make love in a Jacuzzi or a hotel bedroom to add an element of glamour and excitement.

Watch out for a tendency towards escapism around the 15th, when you're at your most vulnerable and sensitive. Just for a few days around the 16th, tough as it might seem, avoid over-indulgence and people who might want to manipulate you for their own ends. By the 18th, you're looking forward to a new-found security and to a Christmas with someone special in your life. Even if it doesn't work out long-term, you at least have the knowledge and self-awareness to know that life and love must always be an adventure for you. And strangely, that's what it's becoming. So don't rush into any seriously long-term commitment just because you think others won't understand you. To be loved for who you are is to be loved because you're a free-range bird and not a battery hen.

Your Love
Horoscope
2004

Capricorn
The Goat

December 21 – January 19

Your Love
Horoscope
2004

Love Check

Why you're fabulous

 You never stop believing in yourself.

 Men can't resist your sensual aura.

Why you're impossible

 You can become too controlling in a relationship.

 Holding back your feelings means no-one really knows where they stand.

Your love secrets

 Erotic conversations beat partying any day.

 You want the best and will often wait forever for the right lover.

 Money and love do go together.

Your sexual style

 Cool to begin with, passionate beneath the sheets.

Who falls for you

Sensitive, needy types who want to be organized, self-starters who like the idea of someone as ambitious as they are, experienced lovers and traditional meat and potatoes men.

Who you fall for

The poet, the stranger, hustlers and non-conformists, or you go to the other extreme and hunt for a man with something classy or classically smooth about him.

You identify with

Bosses, workaholics and people who are honest about their past. Control, realism and a dry sense of humour.

Your greatest temptation

Having sex in the office.

Your greatest strength

Being self-reliant and never depending on anyone.

Passion Profile for 2004

This year you find the incentive to take the plunge, hoping for the long-lasting love that you so crave. But your need for a slow, seductive romance isn't fulfilled quite as quickly as you hope. But March and April bring some delightful romantic encounters, especially at work, which is hardly surprising as you spend so much of your time there. Jupiter's change of direction after May 5 removes the blinkers and shows you the way to true happiness. With Venus's help things will have livened up sexually by July – and by August lust has become your favourite new hobby. Having learnt not to take everything so seriously, you realize that you can write your own recipe for long-term happiness and you're halfway there. If it feels right, don't hold back, and by September one special person could become a major part of your life. Ignore accusations of divided loyalties around the Lunar eclipse at the end of October – you know how much you care. Show it through loving strokes and gentle touches, and take care not to let jealousy come between you and that one man who makes you go weak at the knees.

2004 Month by Month

January

Take some time out to relax on the 7th, when the Full Moon makes you feel like dancing rather than dealing. Socially, you aren't always ready to leap in at the deep end – taking off impulsively to a new venue or meeting up with strangers is not your style – but Mercury's influence in your own sign from the 14th spells communication and a different exchange of interests. Be prepared for a different social life around this time. If you're ready to take the plunge rather than getting defensive or shy – yes, you are often a lot shyer than people realize – then the chances are you'll have the most fabulous fun.

You'll feel like mixing business with pleasure this month and a fascinating conversationalist could turn out to be a double-whammy for success. So make a note of his status, work-wise or not, as this new sexy contact is not to be avoided. Your timing is impeccable when it comes to making the right kind of entrance, and if you need to impress and win over a few close friends to your way of thinking, then wait until after the 21st. Your wit and humour won't go unnoticed and you'll quickly be the centre of attention, especially among those male colleagues who are devoted to your company.

With your ruler Saturn still backtracking slowly through your romantic zone, you're still not sure that Mr Right exists. There may be men out there who are fun to be with but they just don't seem to offer the kind of magic you're looking for. So now's the time to revamp your image and prove that where romantic objectives are concerned you won't settle for second best.

February

You'll be at your most charismatic after the 8th and a seductive gesture from an infiltrator on the work scene on the 12th could put you in touch with someone extra special. Get to know him in your own time and on your own terms. That way you can be sure he's got the patience and integrity to deal with your professional discretion, and also respects your need for diplomacy in relationships.

A close friend could get needy and demanding on the 13th. Any displays of confusion or emotional outbursts in the office or even in the street won't alarm you. Stay cool and be your usual poised and unruffled self – helping out in a crisis is something you manage with complete efficiency, but remember to think about your own needs too, and by the 15th you can turn your attention to your personal happiness again.

And what was it you were thinking about on New Year's Eve? Was it that perhaps this year you were going to cause a stir romantically? Prove that you don't need to live the kind of life that everyone assumes is best for you. One love interest could certainly be provocative around the 18th and give you cause to think seriously about whether or not you're living a lie.

Certain family issues get resolved after the 20th and your inspirational aims and projects for the future will be confirmed as winners by those who can help you realize your dreams.

March

After the Full Moon on the 6th, an amazing man opportunity comes out of the blue. If you're single, a romantic liaison of the spectacular kind is about to take you to the outer limits of sensual heaven. Look out for him at parties and social functions – he's gregarious, powerful and oozes sexiness, so you'll hardly miss him. Do take care if you're already attached – it's not that you're about to create a love triangle, but it does feel as if you're capable of falling into the kind of close liaison which smells of danger. Rather than risk all on a moment's flirtation or a seduction scene, adopt a more down-to-earth approach and divert your energy elsewhere. Perhaps this is the time to test your lover's libido? What with Mars firing up your self-confidence and self-esteem, and the Moon making for sexy nights, you know you've got the motivation and the desire for it. The problem is, can he keep up with your earthy carnal energy? This growing sense of vitality must surely now incite him to a deeper passion and intense sexual desire. He won't resist, but he may insist that you give him a breathing spell before you drag him into that luscious bedroom scenario again.

April

Relationships are always central to your mind and heart, and this month you feel confident that whatever happens in the long run, this April is going to be a special one for you. The Full Moon on the 5th makes you feel secretive and dreamy, so if you're attached this is an excellent time to tell your lover how you truly feel, and if you're single, watch out for that dreamy look in a male colleague's eye. You are now at your most sensuous and loving, so if you are spending all your free weekends with a boyfriend or lover, then, around the 15th, break with tradition for once and suggest doing something you've never done together before. It doesn't have to be radical; it could just be that you roam around a foreign city or have a dirty weekend in the country, but it would make for a few days of extraordinary sensual bliss. If you're single, make sure you get invites to all those parties and business social events. Luck is on your side after the 12th, so go out and find your dream man – it may even be that gorgeous but quietly determined Taurean you know at work.

Whether single or attached, with Mercury backtracking through Taurus most of the month, you might feel a little cynical about romance, but as you well and truly know, that's just a defence because you yearn for that magical never-never land to go on and on. Good old reality, of course, always brings you back down to earth very quickly. But that's because you feel most secure in a relationship which is mutually ambitious, relies on structure and success, and where you can be the power behind your own throne and his, if necessary.

The Sun's move into Taurus on the 20th brings you closer to one love interest than ever before, now you have a renewed faith and belief in him and what he really stands for in your life. This is an important time of year for you when you will begin to feel the power of your own credibility and sense of achievement, both with regard to your personal issues and professional ones. This makes for an excellent time for beginning any new project or working on plans or schemes that needs to be finalized. You both feel emotionally well-balanced and develop a genuinely supportive attitude for each other's success. Shimmering and vivacious, you flirt and enjoy the company of male colleagues, too. So don't feel guilty because you're smiling at the world. In fact, the kind of charm you're radiating is the key to meeting a very important contact for your professional progress.

May

Jupiter's change of direction after the 5th brings you new insight into your passionate nature and you realize that it's time to put happiness on top of your agenda. You're in dazzling form at the beginning of the month and you're lusting after that gorgeous male friend's sexy voice on the 2nd – and by the 7th, with a stroke of luck, you're hearing it on the phone. Take a chance and tell him you're fascinated by his body as well as his mind, especially if you get past the first date.

Watch out that you don't get into a seriously dangerous liaison with the wrong man on the 13th. You're in the mood to take risks, but falling into the arms of someone who's already attached isn't going to make your life any easier.

After the 19th, rational thinking and talking means you can clear the air with a suspicious male friend. He's convinced that you're craving his body, but the chances are you simply like him as a pal. It is in your nature to have intellectual relationships as well as sexual ones. Tell him plainly which it is you want.

A rival's less than flattering remarks won't put you off a minor manhunt on the 22nd. You're at your most vivacious and witty, so he's likely to be attracted to you first anyway. By the end of the month you'll have all the answers or a phone call, and you'll feel confident and charismatic enough to laugh about it too.

If you're attached, May is a month of changeable sexual thoughts.

After the 10th, you feel trapped one moment and totally happy and committed the next. You want to maintain your cool detachment but you also want to feel utterly loved. You need a taste of both or you wouldn't be true to yourself. On the 13th, your lover tells you about his special feelings for you. And it becomes obvious that he wants a deeper commitment. Then on the 14th you're convinced you can maintain your independence and still be a double act. What is it about your ability to bounce back and forth between feelings that keeps you so sane? Facing the reality of your mutual needs becomes a major issue on the 27th and 28th, so make sure you tell yourself the truth and nothing but the truth.

June

You're up for explicit sexual bliss around the 7th. Whatever problems you've recently had with your man, you're beginning to communicate on a deeper level. But a lively social event around the 16th confuses your feelings and you're uncertain whether to retreat quickly from your boyfriend's suspicious gaze or show him how much you care. By the 26th, you'll feel compelled to speak up, whatever the cost. Sexually, you are vibrant and your boyfriend simply can't keep his hands off you. The 21st is the most nerve-racking of days – be careful to put your heart where your mouth is and really mean what you say. He could be assuming that physical involvement means it's serious.

If you're single, a dreamy poetical type is the most likely candidate for your super sexual craving after the 3rd. Watch out for the dazzling, dangerous eyes and listen for the sexy voice on the phone that makes you feel decidedly aroused. An encounter after the 13th with this dreamy stranger puts you in a wanderlust mood for an idyllic affair. Courage is all it takes to make that phone call, but by the 17th you could have feelings of insecurity about your ability to pull this one off without getting hurt. By the 19th, you'll be feeling sensual, romantic and heady with desire. Your emotional and physical allure is at its peak around the same day and you're feeling confident about yourself. Arousal levels reach an all-time high on the 20th, but you aren't sure whether he really understands you. It's time to gently assert your sexual needs, no matter how difficult it is for you. If you do so before the end of the month, you'll sink into his arms and realize he knows exactly what turns you on.

The Sun's move into Cancer on the 21st heralds the summer solstice and brings a few tears to your eyes – either at a weepy film or because you've discovered how close you can become to one special person. And isn't being in love just as painful as falling out of it?

July

You're well and truly steaming with sexiness this month. If you haven't planned your holiday yet do so before the 18th and you'll be on a journey to happiness. On the 1st, be prepared to have to turn down several admirers. They probably wouldn't pass the sensitivity test anyway. Your allure is compelling and high profile, but your vulnerable side is still nudging you to be cautious. What you don't need is to fall head over heels for someone on holiday because you might get hurt. Get yourself noticed before the 21st at an important soiree or 'do' and you'll instantly attract a suave sophisticate. Don't worry, he'll still be there when you get back from your summer break. Absence makes passion grow and grow.

The middle of July is a quiet time for recharging your emotional batteries. Around the New Moon in your own sign on the 17th, you'll wonder how much you've given away about yourself and your sexual needs this summer. And have you only resisted the temptation to lead someone on simply because you're terrified of losing your current man? If you're prepared to flirt dangerously with someone else on the 24th, be careful you don't involve your feelings. You'll soon forget you were tempted by another man, and by the end of the month feelings of tenderness and sexual closeness keep you passionate about your lover.

If you're single, seize the opportunity for a fling on the 8th. You've known he's been interested for some time, and although he didn't actually seem like your perfect man, on second thoughts he might have the kind of wicked charm to keep you amused all night. Here comes seductive Venus to awaken you to a smouldering adventure after the 19th. Don't let a charming rogue deceive you about why he hasn't phoned you yet. He's just playing it cool. Watch out after the 26th for a wistful guru who makes you crave a dreamy relationship. You're just so irresistible this month men can't stop being fascinated by you, so make sure you choose someone who respects your personal needs. Sexually you can't go wrong; hormones are racing, libidos are rising and there's a magical quality about everything you say and do.

August

Creating the perfect lair in which to trap some seriously stunning rogue is top of your agenda this month, thanks to Mars in your adventurous zone from the 10th. And you suddenly realize you have the wit, the power and the necessary seductive skills to create an irresistibly seductive mantrap. What man wouldn't keep coming back for more?

Expect a minor setback on the 11th when Mercury does a U-turn in your chart and you have to make a small sacrifice to keep a family member sweet. Around the New Moon of the 16th, a whole new set of options opens up to you and your time and a romantic desire or wish will be rewarded. Your generosity to those you care about is greatly appreciated and their gratitude and recognition instils you with a burst of new-found confidence. Use that ego-boost, and if you're feeling hemmed in on the 18th, escape into the night. A wild evening shaking your booty and eyeing up the talent will clear cobwebs, shed calories and provide the opportunity for a new sexy friend to escort you home. And with your lair still set, your red-hot companion provides you with an orgasmic night of complete hot summer bliss.

September

Get involved in teamwork or join in group activities around the 3rd, when Venus supplies seductive skills aplenty for you to lead the way in work and pleasure. You might notice that someone in the group is paying special attention to you, but is he interested in what you have to say or what you have hidden beneath your shirt? Have you considered that it could be both? You might be tempted to be frosty on the 5th, especially if you allow yourself to get distracted by practical issues. Do that and you'll miss the chance of a sizzlingly passionate encounter of the physical kind. Venus moves into your sexual zone on the 6th, bringing a string of sensual offers. Pick the man who wants your mind as well as your body. Good sex is fine, but a little communication in between can move you into the realms of a deeper and more stable relationship.

With Jupiter's challenging influence, you know it's time to seriously commit yourself to one long-standing relationship, or give it up. Confusion reigns for the first two weeks of the month and your lover's unreliability around the 19th will make you wonder if it's worth the bother. By the 25th, you realize that the perfect man doesn't exist. Start loving him for his imperfections and by the 28th you'll have a much clearer perspective of how to work at this relationship and make it a success. Throughout the month you'll be faced with a string of potential lovers. So enjoy the attention of all those lone-wolves; flirt, date and don't feel you have to commit yourself to anyone yet. Romantically you also want some fun, so enjoy those nights out. And you never know, all that sparkling energy could make Mr Unreliable buck his ideas up.

October

Novelty and change are what you're hankering for all month and you're willing to put in the groundwork to make things happen. With Venus in Virgo from the 3rd until the 28th, you'll reinvent unsatisfactory relationships and come up with ways to spice up your love life.

Clear out the dead wood before the 14th, when the Solar eclipse puts the blinkers on your romantic intuition. It could leave you believing that feelings of lust are the real thing. It's highly likely that they're not, so try not to declare undying love or it could lead to heartbreak. You won't have much time to worry about it as Venus brings a string of sexy hunks, like moths to a flame, blinded by your dynamic aura. Don't be surprised when a gorgeously persistent one wants more than just a quick fling – and indulge your cravings for lust and luxury on the 17th.

On the 25th, you might be disappointed by the negativity of the one man you really care for. It's simply that due to the Lunar eclipse he suspects he has divided loyalties. So remember, he's only feeling vulnerable. And by the end of the month the delightful influences of the Sun and Jupiter bring a greater feeling of happiness and satisfaction than you've experienced in a long time. Share that warmth, snuggle up to your lover and show him just how generous and charming you can be when you're appreciated.

November

You've a twinkle in your eye from the 11th, thanks to the magical influence of Mars in sexy Scorpio providing you with more than your fair share of male attention. You're looking and feeling a million dollars, and Mercury's leap into dynamic Sagittarius gives you the seductive charms of a *femme fatale*, resulting in a spectacular meeting of body and mind. Beauty is of utmost importance during this phase, so look out for that perfectly formed torso down at the gym or jogging through the park and impress him with your own sleek image and cool allure.

On the 16th, you're filled with emotional energy but are quite likely to squander it. Just take care you don't play too many games – even though you're very controlled about your feelings, there are moments when you just have to express yourself and it could all come out the wrong way. If you're attached then it might mean a few nights of silent anger; if you're single, you might feel that no-one understands you and want to hide in the corner or curl up with your favourite book. So curb that stubborn streak and by the Full Moon on the 26th you'll be feeling impulsive and ready to be honest enough to share your true thoughts.

Venus provides you with the seductive drive and motivation to attract that man who makes you melt after the 23rd – and with the Sun moving into your secret zone on the 21st, you have no choice but to reveal your romantic intentions, otherwise you'll never know what he really thinks about you.

December

Recent discoveries have given you magical powers of self-knowledge and a greater understanding of how much people value you. You're so deep in thought you might not notice that a sultry rogue has his eyes on you. Be sure to keep yourself free for a sizzling date around the New Moon on the 12th. Forget the past and look ahead. Go on a spree for an outfit that accentuates your best assets and that sexy rogue won't be able to keep his eyes off you. Remember though that you deserve the best and don't take anything less. Your high ideals are hard to live up to around the 14th and he might feel he's going to be trapped. Try to ignore the spin that Mercury's U-turn in your chart puts on everything until the 20th and remember that your down-to-earth self-belief is far more important than any wild promises and Christmas fantasies about long-term commitment, especially when what you both need is some fun and space.

After the 21st, the Sun's move into your own sign brings enthusiastic new people into your life, inspiring you with ideas and seductive offers. Enjoy the festive spirit, but beware of over-extravagance around the 25th. It might make you popular, but your natural charm and popularity doesn't need to be bought. People love you without the baubles. Dazzle them with your charm and exploit your natural gifts. If you're single, this is your chance to be exploited in the most deliciously enjoyable way by the end of the year.

If you're feeling confused on the 28th, wherever you are, use all your powers of persuasion to convince your lover that the way forward is together. You're both a force to be reckoned with and this is your chance to make a successful twosome. So make the end of the year one when emotionally, physically and materially you both know that you are on the road to a fantastic future together. All it takes is to open up about your true needs and true love will be all yours.

Aquarius

The Water-bearer

January 20 – February 18

Love Check

Why you're fabulous

- When you dedicate yourself to a cause, you'll never give up the campaign.
- You believe in independence and don't resent your man his freedom.
- Because you're a sexual maverick men drool after you.

Why you're impossible

- You ask for things you want in a very roundabout way.
- You often make irritatingly radical statements just to wind him up.

Your love secrets

- Beneath that cool intellect is a very romantic soul.
- You can feel jealous, even though you always deny it.
- You ask for sex in the most outrageously public places, just to shock him and everyone else.

Your sexual style

- Cool, experimental and different for the sake of being different.

Who falls for you

- Conventional business tycoons, rugged backpacking types who want you to go on safari with them, conformists who see everything in life as a personal battle or victory.

Who you fall for

- Rogue mavericks, men who think about the universe more than themselves, freedom-lovers with witty brains and glamorous, successful entrepreneurs.

You identify with

- Freedom, cosmopolitan friends, men who aren't interested in commitment, humanitarian types who save whales but surf waves in their free time.

Your greatest temptation

- Telling him you have the all answers when he hasn't any questions.

Your greatest strength

- Knowing that universal love does make the world go round.

Passion profile for 2004

From January through to March, you're feeling far more passion-ate about life and love than you have for a long time. You're on a sexual high and because you are convinced you know what you want, every man you meet finds you seductively challenging. But this year's cosmic line-up forces you to realize that maybe you've been deceiving yourself and, in fact, you're not putting your own ideals and values first. Perhaps you've been living your life according to family or friends' expectations about your role in relationships? Yet what other people assume is right for you is not really in line with your true ideals. It's time to be true to yourself, rather than trying to be someone you're not. Mars moves into your relationship zone on June 24 and you have to confront the fact that unless you live by your own beliefs and principles you can never feel really secure with anyone else. Throughout the summer you flirt, seduce and attract the most delicious attention without a care in the world. No longer needy, negative or demanding, by December you're far more optimistic about love, but, most importantly, you realize your independence is sacred. With self-love comes a whole new attitude to relating, and by the end of the year Jupiter brings you the romantic happiness and sexual bliss you truly crave.

2004 Month by Month

January

Remember that self-respect is essential if you're going to find true equality in your relationships. And this month you begin to take advantage of your cool, aloof and enigmatic image. Of course you have to care about others, but revel for once in your growing self-esteem and be the centre of attention. A hunch about how easy it is to make someone close to you happy gives you a new sense of responsibility towards your friends and yourself. With Mercury moving forward in your chart, you can expand your ideas, widen your vision for new romantic opportunities and enjoy the changes that are forcing you to develop a greater sense of freedom. Now is the time to unbind yourself from past commitments that have been wearing you down. Establish a new set of rules – ones you have created for yourself – and stick to them.

You've been fascinated by so many changes in your work environment of late and you're now prepared to make a firm commitment to pursue an exciting new venture. And an in-house meeting around the 15th gives you the opportunity to meet someone who could have a considerable effect on you, both physically and mentally. But you could also feel that one admirer isn't being honest with their feelings about a future venture and it's wise to wait until after the 25th before forcing an issue or taking a chance to speak up yourself. Whatever you say then can only add to your charisma, so be prepared to offer worthwhile advice and support rather than simply hearsay.

By the middle of the month your careful analysis of your own romantic motivations will have paid off and you'll feel vivacious and energized, thanks to the New Moon in your own sign on the 21st. Carefree and liberated, you're ready for a fun-packed social life. Friends or lovers confirm your fabulous allure on the 23rd and by the 30th your fantastic sex appeal attracts an array of delicious flirtations. Now you're at your most cool and glamorous there's a chance that your inspiring conversation could bring you the attention and success you deserve.

February

There'll be some adrenalin-racing moments around the 6th and, if you're single, you'll feel in the mood for a relationship adventure. With Mercury in your own sign from the 7th and your ruler Uranus breaking the ice with Mercury later on in the month, there's a chance that someone who you never thought could possibly take an interest in you most certainly has.

If you're attached, then talking openly about your feelings and future plans with your partner won't go amiss this month. Sometimes you need to express your wildest of dreams just to ensure that others know you do have direction and complete authority over your own life. Asserting your needs is essential if you want to maintain the status quo within your relationship. However much you value your independence, there are times when you need the support and advice of the one person you trust.

Staking your claim in a new idea and backing it puts you closer to someone with credibility around the 16th. This is the kind of man who you can trust as a friend, but don't make judgements about his taste in clothes before he's had time to change for dinner.

Take the opportunity on the 18th to prove how special, dedicated and motivated you really are to the people that count. Feelings of self-doubt could put you temporarily off track on the 22nd, but you'll have snapped out of it by the 29th. Now you can leap forward and change your approach to relationships. Think it through carefully and make use of your analytical mind. You need to maintain your freedom, yet you want a close relationship. Remember, independence and commitment aren't necessarily mutually exclusive. And perhaps in your frantic desire to find Mr Right you've been unconsciously frightening off potential partners because you've appeared too needy. Now you can show you are self-possessed and self-assured.

March

If you're single, internet connections seem to be taking up a lot of your time and you feel at last that being Miss Independent does have its advantages. You have choices, a range of possible dates and a variety of new male and female friends. Just take care you really find out as much as you can about your contacts before you set off to meet them. One could turn out to be utterly disappointing around the 10th, but another seems almost 'too good to be true' that you decide to delete him from your message box. Don't make impulsive choices this month – Mars brings you the chance for romantic adventure.

If you're attached, around the 7th is an excellent time to sign, seal or deliver that important message to a boyfriend. You could either e-mail him or write a letter, but face to face is even better for rewarding conversation – you know how you love to be mentally stimulated. He really needs some mind-expanding awareness, and if you keep it physically-motivated rather than merely intellectual, you can now establish a fabulous rapport. With Mars entering the area of your chart concerning romance, adventurous sex and fascinating strangers, remember that committing yourself to only one man is often an Aquarian dilemma. Remind your boyfriend that intimacy knows no bounds as long as he remembers to give you your space. Loyalty is a personal dream on the other hand, and being devoted to all your friends as well as your man with equal love and dedication is now the message you need to put across. You trust and believe in him, so it's time for him to trust and believe in you.

Sort out a minor lover's tiff on the 15th, particularly if you're forced to make compromises concerning your career. You start to feel as if those changes you were planning in your relationship are all about to fall through. Don't worry, there's an opportunity to air your feelings on the 20th and discover your dynamic sexual libido hasn't been wasted. It's time to truly shine. Sexually, you feel that it's time to improvize with your man. If you're into experimenting, then speak up on the 23rd, and by the 30th you'll be wondering why you'd never suggested that technique before.

April

Your desire for a good social life could be upset by the preoccupations of others with themselves, especially those who might consider you easy prey. Your open and altruistic nature draws many desperados to your side, so be wise and sort out exactly who it is you can trust.

Watch out you don't put your foot in it after the 18th – sharing your more radical thoughts to an associate could turn out to be seriously provocative. Your reputation isn't at stake, but enjoying yourself is. Instead, indulge in the company of friends who truly understand your zaniest of ideas.

With Venus moving forward through the area of your chart concerning high romance from the 4th, you'll feel ready to start listening to what others have to say and clarify an issue surrounding a lack of communication that involves your relationship with either a close friend or business associate. This is one month when it's important to listen to someone else's input, otherwise you could become muddled and your thoughts confused. Don't worry, you'll have a clear head and a clear conscience by the end of the month. The Full Moon on the 5th vitalizes your energy levels and you'll feel at your most glamorous and enigmatic. Charisma is your ally, so use every available moment to impress and stun your way to happiness.

You have now reached a point in your close intimate relationships where maintaining your independence is essential for achieving your long-term goals. Remember that it's your pride rather than necessity which prevents you sometimes from opening up your heart, so take the last week of April to experience a deeper understanding of your fears and joys and it should prove to be one of the most exciting and romantically exhilarating ever.

May

You're in tigress form this month and your eyes will be hunting on the 4th. If you're single, tell a sexy stranger your life story on the 15th and you won't be disappointed by his reactions. A decidedly dreamy male colleague could propose more than a simple date after the 19th. He may not be the sexiest man around, but he is magnetic and certainly intriguing. Don't avoid him, he could turn out to be more arousing than you imagined.

If you're attached, you're at your most irresistible and glamorous. In fact, your boyfriend just can't have enough of you on the 12th. Use the time to plan your future summer break if you haven't already done so. Romantic locations are best otherwise you might get led astray by social temptations of the male kind. Sexual dreams become reality for you both on the 17th, so take care you keep your physical attraction passionate and warm. Feelings of doubt about your deepest desires could surface by the end of the month. On the 30th, you'll have to make some kind of compromise between making a commitment and letting him know you can't be certain of anything right now.

If you're single, there is someone special you've had your eye on for some time. He could be the kind who could charm the birds out of the trees, but you're finding it difficult to make yourself understood. By the 25th, you're feeling confused about whether to search for a close and permanent involvement or simply to enjoy yourself and keep your sexual independence. By the 29th, your partying mood transforms your sense of what love is all about – you want to be desired for your charismatic qualities, both physically and emotionally. Perhaps you can finally find someone who will give you the freedom to be you.

June

Mars surges into your ambitious territory and the Sun's direction helps get your creative juices flowing, so get to work and show off your talents. You're meeting influential high-flyers all month and someone wants to see you in print. No, not Penthouse centrefold, they like the way you express yourself, literally. With Jupiter's help, success can be found in publishing or further education. Listen to any advice you can get, enter competitions and take an evening class to hone your skills and meet like-minds in prime, intellectual hunk territory. Around the 19th, don't let the Venus-Jupiter square make you impetuous. Work within your limits and don't imagine yourself launching the adult answer to Harry Potter quite yet. Use this glamorous world of ideas and Jupiter's influence to impress a handsome rogue instead. Is he interested in you or your hidden talents, and, frankly, do you care? Find common ground, get to know him better and then show him some sensual talents you've kept hidden for weeks.

Mars moves forward into your relationship zone on the 24th, lending you the wit and charm to sparkle at parties, wowing a string of sexy blokes. You're being seduced by an easy life of past loves and present *beaux*. Prioritize your time. Intersperse important projects with deliciously sexy frolics whenever you can fit them into your busy schedule. You now begin to see the new you is so much better than the old you. And what's so wonderful is that your values are becoming clearer. You don't have to pretend to be something you're not and you are beginning to appreciate how important it is to love yourself.

July

Blissful pleasure beckons after the 5th and you'll feel magical, wicked and ready for any romantic escapades. Mercury's move into your relationship zone on the 5th puts everything at last in perspective regarding a boyfriend. On the 8th, expect to seduce him out there in public if you have to prove your point. Watch out after the 16th that you don't cause a major conflict. Wisely stop flirting before your boyfriend gets that green-eyed monster look. There's a seductive twinkle in your boyfriend's eye on the 18th and you're eager to tell him how you truly feel. The reality of who's going to clean the bath or make the next meal are pressing problems, but sexual urgency comes higher on the list right now. You sexually crave more passion after the 25th. Your adrenalin levels are high and the early summer sun is making you feel aroused. Once you've cleared the air you can enjoy some moments of exquisite tenderness, especially on the 26th.

If you're single, the 11th sees you glowing with outrageous confidence. You'll be feeling passionate and orgasmic on the 18th, so make sure it's with someone who can match your incredible adrenalin levels. You fall in love with a beautiful body on the 22nd. But forget about his mind and just enjoy the visual feast while it lasts. You're romantically enflamed again on the 29th when a passing entrepreneur or gorgeous colleague notices your charismatic personality. Cool your own passion, he's actually already attached. Challenging moments occur the following day when a social climber pushes a few sexual buttons and you just can't resist his attention.

It's one of those months for close emotional rapport with a sexy male colleague, but you could find all that possessive side of his nature a little scary. You are feeling extra vulnerable, so don't waste time. Explain you are always ready to share your mind, but never your body.

August

Twinges of emotional disappointment rear their head on the 2nd when thoughts of a past affair haunt you. Don't vent your anger or blame those nearest to you for feelings you've suppressed. If your current *amour* doesn't invoke fervent violins, crashing waves and all that true love and passion suggests, it's a problem you must solve. It's tough being a perfectionist, but you are, so strive for your ideal. Did someone from the past pull at all the right strings or are you remembering events with rose-tinted spectacles? By the New Moon of the 16th, you're determined to find out for sure and so is your long-lost *amour*. Enhance your sensuous night of passion with an element of intrigue. Arrange a clandestine rendezvous and show him how much you want him, silently, with every inch of your body. Kiss him in all those familiar erogenous places – and remember that you need romance as much as anyone else and the reality of love is in the here and now, not in past escapades. After Mercury moves forward again on the 25th, decide whether you want crashing waves or safety.

Don't lose the chance of true happiness for fear of losing face. With Pluto's change of direction on the 30th everyone will want a part of you, but only you can decide who to share yourself with. Be utterly selfish and head for dinner *a deux* with one lover who makes you hear music even when the turntable's bare.

September

A flirtatious encounter with a charismatic property dealer around the 7th gains you the upper hand, or is it just Venus in your negotiating zone urging you to drive a hard bargain? Either way, use your dazzling smile and sex appeal to get the flat, the man or whatever you want most. Ignore any twinges of negativity. With Jupiter on your side you can't fail. Even if you're longing for the impossible, at least the possibilities are actually endless this month.

And the idealistic moves of Jupiter and Mars into Libra from the 25th makes you realize you want more – and you deserve it. Set your aims high and don't ever put yourself down or try to be something you're not.

If there's a sexy rogue you've been dying to bag, he'll find it impossible not to fall for your wily, seductive charms. With the help of Venus from the 8th, make your lair a temple to passion. Dot candles around the room, burn scented oils and play CD's that make him tingle with desire. Around the 24th, you need to feel pampered and it's his turn to come up with ways of reaching new heights of sexual intensity. Watch out, he's more imaginative than you thought.

October

Your desire for excitement will be completely fulfilled by a whirl of glamorous events putting you in the spotlight all month. Your ruler Uranus gives you the chance to write the script and play leading role on the 1st, and isn't that just how you like it? Take centre stage and make a deep connection with a gorgeous hunk who wants to play your leading man. Go way beyond the first kiss when you get him behind the scenes. Around the 14th, the Solar eclipse increases your sense of drama, so don't get jealous if he fraternizes with a minor player. It's not serious and if you blow it out of proportion you'll be dumped by your romantic lead. Around the 22nd, you're determined to win. You will, and with the Lunar eclipse of the 28th you're willing to take things further than most. Get Romeo backstage and show him just how desirable you are. Stroke his body all over and you never know, he might even cook you breakfast. By the end of the month he'll be climbing your balcony every night.

Neptune's change of direction at the end of the month causes confusion over your true aspirations. Listen to your heart, be yourself and don't give into any twinges of doubt. They have no place in your life.

November

Don't ditch your nearest and dearest for a fascinating maverick who'll blind you with his charms around the 9th. With your ruler Uranus moving forward from the 11th, you can't resist a man with sex appeal and this one's got it oozing from every pore. But why is someone so perfect not already snapped up? You may find he is but he's willing to share himself around. But are you willing to play second fiddle? Around the 11th, Mars moves into deceptive Scorpio to show just how unreliable he can be. Take his declarations with a pinch of salt and don't be persuaded to part with your heart.

On the 14th, an away-from-it-all break or change in routine will give you the time to decide what you want from your relationship, but it's not as clear cut as you think. The Sun's move into Sagittarius on the 21st heralds a streak of perversity and a desire to go against the grain. Pushing the boundaries is one thing, but imposing your will on others is another. Don't expect anyone to follow your orders and neither should you follow theirs. Except of course after the 22nd, when Venus moves into your empowering zone, and you might be tempted into testing out a little playful bondage with a lover who puts your needs first. Get the cuffs on him – this one sounds too good to let go.

December

Christmas party antics are starting early and you're sure a sexy rogue has set his compass in your direction. And who can blame him? The Sun enhances your vivacious nature and he can't resist the way you light up a room. You'll be connecting on all levels around the 4th, and one of them is a highly charged sexual one.

The Sun's relationship to passionate Pluto this month changes the dynamics of one close relationship, bringing dramatic upheavals in your love life. Drama is your forte, but it's tough for those involved to rationalize your actions. Go with it, whether you decide to stick with the new or return to the tried and tested. By the 10th you'll know that the decision you've made is the right one.

The Sun and Jupiter brings you romantic wealth, success and great contentment, and you'll be ending the year in emotional and sexual bliss. You've come a long way and your disposition towards one lover is sweeter than ever. Could it be the real thing? Either way, around the 17th you'll be putting every effort into making it work. Santa's kind this year. What more could you want for Christmas than a loving, sensual relationship with a man who's hotter than a log fire. Keep him well-stoked and he won't stop burning with desire for your seductive charms well into the new year.

Pisces

The Fish

February 19 – March 20

Love Check

Why you're fabulous

 Sensitive and imaginative, you are the goddess of romance.

 You always care about your true friends.

 You rarely argue and are always the peacemaker.

Why you're impossible

 Rather than face reality, you prefer to live in a dream world.

 You often play the blame-game to defend your vulnerable side.

Your love secrets

 You need someone to understand your changeable nature.

 You're often confused about your role in a relationship.

 A sensitive, compassionate lover makes you feel truly adored.

Your sexual style

 Hypnotic, dreamy and always seductive.

Who falls for you

 Visionary dreamers, addictive personality types who want you to save them and refined, rational intellectuals who are hooked by your romantic personality.

Who you fall for

 Physically beautiful men, perfectionists, priests, gurus and musicians, loners who want to be rescued and mystery men who won't tell you anything about their life.

You identify with

 Mystics, actors and martyrs. Healing, theatre, films and the imagination.

Your greatest temptation

 Drifting off into a dream world rather than facing the reality of phoning him.

Your greatest strength

 Coming to the rescue when he's got problems.

Passion Profile for 2004

The only one doing any dumping this year is you, and the most important thing being dumped are your doubts, thanks to Jupiter's influence right through until September, bringing enlightenment to the way you relate. January brings roses and romance and February some pretty steamy action. Rediscovering realms of sexual intimacy is a major boost to your ego all through spring. In late May, something or someone from the past brings awareness to the present and you begin to realize how to deal with your deepest desires. June, and the cosmos, clarifies your thoughts and you know that you couldn't be happy with anything which wasn't wholly emotionally satisfying. A new path begins on June 21 and a fantastic opportunity occurs to change your romantic life to the way you've longed for for so long. With so many planets cruising through the flirty, romantic part of your chart from September till the end of the year, expect heaps of light-hearted fun. Often, just when you stop looking for that fairytale romance, it comes looking for you. By December, admire what you're achieving. You've faced your dragons and you've come a long way, but the real excitement has only just begun.

2004 Month by Month

January

Every close sexual relationship for you is a mysterious and some-times tangled web of desire, passion and excitement. Recently you've not only had the chance to show how you feel about some-one special, but you've also reassured yourself about how much someone truly cares about and considers you. You're in the mood for a closer intimacy with your man after the 9th, when Venus makes you crave closeness and sexual euphoria. Feelings of doubt could have crept into your mind recently about whether he's truly the ultimate love of your life, so think clearly and open your heart to your true feelings. The Full Moon on the 7th tempts you to do something totally different, whether it's simply to be more forward about putting your desires across to him or actually suggesting an expedition of a lifetime. Whether you impulsively take off for a hike around the Andes or just a leisurely jaunt to the park or your favourite restaurant, make this a week when you feel a renewed sense of confidence about making a deliberate choice.

Being so acutely aware of other people's moods, you could feel insecure about your future long-term plans around the 11th, when there's an air of frustration in your personal life. By the 26th, you'll realize this was only a temporary but important blip to open you up to a new and creative way of thinking.

The New Moon on the 21st makes you feel like seeing old friends or family, or simply spending a night in with your boyfriend and reliving romantic moments.

February

After the 6th you'll feel ready to express all those secret thoughts you've been keeping to yourself this month. With Uranus's intriguing influence in your own sign, make sure you only open up to those you can really trust. Telling others your future plans could prove a problem on the 13th, so keep your mouth firmly closed and don't mention a word to a soul until you are sure that your schemes are definitely going to be followed through.

Fantasy and escaping from reality play a big part in your life this month, with Mercury in your daydreaming zone. You'll be in the mood for clandestine romance, secret messages to your boyfriend or indulging in sexual fantasies. With a New Moon in your own sign on the 20th, you feel dizzy with in-loveness again. If you're attached, a boyfriend sees you in a shimmering new light. If you're single, be at your most scintillating and look out for a wonderful rogue on the staircase. You'll be on your way up to heaven as soon as you've gazed into his eyes. All those dreams are beginning to tell you something. Are you truly ready to play an invisible role in someone else's life, or are you ready now to break out of the feelings of confinement or exile and start to live life more openly and with energy?

Take care around the 22nd when you may feel like sinking into a cosy chair and vegetating for a month – it's all so exhausting you really would rather chill out than eat out. But listen to your heart, it's there you'll find the answers.

Mars highlights your finances after the 12th and you can take the opportunity to splash out on yourself for once. With a bonus or extra cash in your wallet you could feel in the mood to spend it all on friends. Entertaining others is a pleasure for you this month, but think carefully about your budget before you get too extravagant. Seize the opportunity to look after 'number one' for a change, rather than being generous to those who could turn out to be users or time-wasters.

March

You've been living in a dreamier world than ever before, but now that Uranus and Neptune are changing gear, those feelings of not living out your true potential suddenly change and you begin to have a clearer picture of where you are going in your life again and who you are going with.

As Saturn moves forward again through your romantic zone from the 7th, flirtatious gestures from colleagues or friendly rogues makes you more sexually confident than ever. But feelings and emotions run deep for you now and it looks like you're about to catch the relationship bug. If you're single, keep your eyes wide open and by the 20th candidates should come running thick and fast. Venus brings you not only a new man or a new sense of pleasure, but also new values about your own image in other people's eyes. Now you can begin to see how you appear to others and have a refined and fresher clarity of vision about your own needs and values in a relationship.

If you already have a man, then this month is a time for libido peaks, sexual surrender and passionate encounters. Mars's move into your power zone makes you feel deliciously wicked after the 21st. Plan a night of deep and languorous sensuality with your man, or be wildly romantic and spontaneous and go out for a date under the stars. You can now plan future projects or travel plans together and enjoy the company of friends without any heckling or tantrums – from the friends that is. You've found the past few months that others have come to depend on your compassion and willingness to listen to their troubles, but now you can have some peace and redirect your energies to yourself, your creative talents and your lover.

April

Your extraordinary capacity to be available for everyone else's crisis reverses after the 18th when a rival's complex love triangle means she's not pulling her weight at work and you begin to get noticed for your talents by VIP contacts. Light-hearted flirtations abound and you feel amused, entertained and literally on your toes. Be extra beguiling towards those in power.

You have an incredible talent for bewitching any man, whether he's your current lover or just the boss. First of all, wisely impress the boss by sorting out a mega conflict of egos down the corridor. And while your knack for problem-solving is inspiring those around you, let a friend confide in you about a romantic obsession. Their insights, experiences and perhaps even their rejects could be of great use for your own personal quest later on in the year. And what about your lover? Well, by the 25th you can finally escape all those heavy office political debates and share lingering gazes across a candlelit dinner instead.

If you're single, enjoy a flirtatious or clandestine weekend around the 10th, when you'll have some sexy or volatile moments with a romantic rogue. However sensitive you are to his passion for you, he's not the right man for you for anything other than a quick fling. You are sexually at your most stunning, so choose your men carefully and with discretion. You don't need one-night stands in your life right now, however much you want male company and love. Mercury's change of emphasis on the 30th makes you feel ready to change your outlook on men in general, whether it's for a raunchy adventure or simply to establish a friendship.

May

At the beginning of the month your mystique is enhanced by Venus's moves and you'll have a more vitalized and magical aura to bring you instant man appeal. Various colleagues ask you out on dates around the 4th and you can't make up your mind whether to go out and have fun just for the sake of it or sit around dreaming about Mr Right. But it's time to be spontaneous rather than try to plot your tactics. You won't even have time to decide whether to phone an admirer you meet at a social 'do' around the 9th, because he'll be on the hunt for you. Just take care that you remain enigmatic and elusive if you want to catch your rogue. This could be the beginning of a new romantic fling, so celebrate your affair with fresh self-belief and seduce him with your sensual mystique all night long to bring you a truly magical change of fortune.

If you're attached and your boyfriend has been too eager to set the pace or assume your opinions are similar to his, now's the time to reveal what your true values are. The New Moon on the 19th makes for deeply passionate moments. Sexually, you can use this powerful moonlit energy to escape into sensual euphoria. Turn the light out and if the night's clear, let the Moon light up your embrace.

Usually added financial responsibilities fill you with horror, yet the last week of May makes you feel optimistic about the future and ready to take on new commitments. Reality is still a necessity to you, however much you'd rather escape to some fantasy world, or at the very least a desert island with your favourite gorgeous man. But deep in your heart you know that you also have to make some choices regarding an ex-lover who seems intent on getting you back. Were his feelings for you as genuine as you'd like them to be, and were you playing a role just to keep him? By the end of the month you realize that you can't go on dwelling on the past. So make it clear that you have your own boundaries and your own individuality, and you will not return to a relationship where you had to pretend to be something you're not.

June

Luckily your charisma is just oozing sexual attraction after the 8th, so you'll be pursued by gorgeous hunks more interested in physical contact than long-drawn-out seduction scenarios. Phone calls, mind games and mild flirtations just don't seem to get close to your body, let alone your libido. You're at your most compelling on the 20th – passionate, poised and oh so sexy. You'll be feeling ready to make new connections by the 25th. Especially after you experience wicked moments with a gorgeous rogue. Check out his eyes. If they're green, go wild; if they're chillingly blue, avoid him altogether.

If you're attached, around the 4th your boyfriend reminds you that love is all about sharing that last glass of wine. You're dizzy with desire on the 7th, but you're left feeling frustrated because he's so busy working and planning his future he misses the opportunity to play. Sexual arousal becomes a deeply sensuous experience on the 18th and by the 20th you wonder which aphrodisiac he's been lacing your drink with. Take the time out on the 26th and 27th to concentrate on future relationship plans rather than brooding on past mistakes. You've been hurt once, but this time make sure your choice is right. You're ready to speak up, but the words just don't come out right. Don't worry, by the end of the month you'll be sure that he knows how you feel anyway.

If you're single, the 17th or 18th are excellent days to seduce a flirtatious but smooth operator. In-house romantic entertainment with a new *amour* could prove more pleasurable than you ever imagined after the 20th. He's not your type but he does seem to know where to touch you in all the most sizzling places. You begin to wonder about a holiday romance. Choosing your destination isn't easy. If you've already booked, then watch out for a stranger with a wide grin – he could be ready for a quick fling. Go for it, as long as you are aware of the consequences. You might never want to return home.

July

If you're attached, you'll feel like breaking the ice on the 2nd and you'll reveal a few saucy secrets to your boyfriend. You'll be ready to launch yourself into a different way of communicating your sexual needs on the 4th. So tell him the sexual positions you adore best of all, instead of assuming he knows what turns you on. After the 7th, you're seriously thinking of a long-term relationship with him. But the trouble is you keep changing your mind this month and he keeps his thoughts to himself. Physically you know he's infatuated with you, but around the 15th you don't know whether to get more involved or get out quick. One minute you can't get enough of him, the next you feel uncertain about your libido. Don't worry, the feelings will pass by the 17th when you realize you've fallen in deeper than you intended.

You're wondering why he needs more sleep, especially on the 19th and 20th when you're sexually at your peak and he can't resist your high sex drive. But it's tiring him out. After the 22nd you cool down a bit – well, long enough to take a shower alone instead of always together. Rationalize your feelings for him. You're ready to tell him how and why your relationship could improve. It's not that you don't like things the way they are, only you need to have some sense of where you are going. You know he sexually craves you but he hasn't actually said he wants a long-term relationship. By the end of the month you begin to realize there's no point pushing him because he'll only get cold feet. Play the game his way.

If you're single, there's no time like the present to get your message across, especially after the 7th when your allure is seductive, sultry and totally wicked. On the 22nd, expect a cheeky, flirtatious phone call to get your pulse racing. Quiet contemplation about those men in your life who've been important to you fills your mind after the 25th. Dreaming of ex's isn't exactly your style, but analyzing what went wrong and what went right confirms your own sense of self-esteem. After the 27th, you'll be feeling sexy, radiant and poised enough to tantalize the smouldering rogue who enters that office door.

August

Money, money, money is a major aphrodisiac to your security-loving streak, and thanks to Jupiter's ego-boosting energy on the 10th you're in an excellent position to feel rich in body, mind and spirit. Whether you're dabbling in shares or buying and selling property, lucky Jupiter helps you to succeed, especially around the New Moon on the 16th. And do you know how sexy it makes you? Impeccable grooming adds to your golden glow of success, attracting a queue of charismatic, wealthy hunks who want to ply you with champagne and woo you in style, while Venus cruises your partying zone from the 7th.

Friends are vying for your company this month, but from the 10th all you'll want to do is to cosy up with your dream lover. Does he know that a weekend by the water will turn you into a rampant sea nymph? Show him how. Thanks to Mars tracking through your relationship zone after the 10th, you have the chance to spice up your lovemaking with a midnight skinny-dip. Show him how much you're turned on, then find yourselves a secluded cove, pool or Jacuzzi and make passionate underwater love, ebbing and flowing in time with the waves.

September

Light-hearted conversations and discreet enquiries will help you to discover whether the rogue who's coming on strong is getting serious or just up for a quick fling. The old-fashioned girl in you just can't help but want more, so enjoy the moment and you might find it's you who doesn't want to commit.

The New Moon of the 14th brings party invitations whizzing through the letterbox and you're having such a good time you want it to last forever. Venus gives you a ravishing quality, attracting bundles of romantic encounters and sexy offers from the 8th. You're given an opportunity for fabulous sex and great wealth, but could that just be a projection of what you think you want? A rare Jupiter-Mars link on the 26th enhances less superficial ideals and dreams, so don't lose sight of your deeper, more spiritual desires.

Watch out that a deeply-fuelled passion for a virile rogue doesn't make you over-possessive mid-month, with Mars in the emotional zone of your chart you could find yourself in all sorts of trouble. It may have been the best one-off love affair of your life, but at what cost? Escape from it all and by the 28th you'll see a clearer picture. Put strangers and their warped desires through the shredder and get back to more nourishing, well-rounded relationships with those who deserve your special love.

If you're attached, you feel that your partner is gaining respect for your emotional honesty. Yet your own suspicions are on red alert and you can't be sure of his motives for wanting you. You've been through the cauldron of love's swirling passions enough times to know that you have no choice but to make sure this relationship is right for you. With Mars's confrontational influence in your chart this month, there's still a dilemma between your need for a transformative, mind-blowing partnership and his 'wait and see' approach to relationships. So live for the moment, be honest about what you want, but give him time to understand you.

October

Someone you thought was just a friend becomes more than a shoulder to cry on as you start sharing your intimate secrets. Allowing your emotional vulnerability to show is irresistible to a knight in shining armour. Around the Solar eclipse of the 14th, a more passionate relationship should develop and you can't keep your hands off each other. With Venus in the expressive area of your chart, excite him with imaginative sexual suggestions but let him take the lead – after all, he's the hero. Put him on a pedestal, tell him how big and strong he is, and get him to prove that he's also tender, romantic and your personal bodyguard. The transition from friend to lover is tough and the eclipse of the Moon on the 28th will make you wonder if you've made a mistake. But it will give you time to think things through properly and rationally.

By the end of the month you'll have swapped your serious aspirations for the pursuit of fun. Your new-found air of liberation will be so arousing you'll be pursued by all those admirers who once may have thought you easy prey. Don't allow yourself to be caught, but enjoy the pleasures of seduction without the pressures of long-term commitment.

November

Watch out, there'll be a swarm of rogues queuing to get you alone, while Mercury's sparkling influence has you scribbling raunchy e-mails and spouting saucy remarks until the 18th. You're at your naughtiest around the 11th, when Mars zooms into your adventurous zone and triggers off a perfect time to begin a scorching flirtation, especially where a sexy Scorpio's involved. In fact, Venus in Scorpio after the 22nd raises your sex life to explosive levels and gives you the opportunity to try something outrageously different. Check out a movie on a late-night channel together – it's a surprising turn on and can give you ideas for games you've only dreamed of. You'll find yourself fascinated by men you meet through your work or bump into in pubs, coffee bars or down the delicatessen, when surprise encounters are highlighted by Mercury's interactive influence. A man in a flashy car and a designer jacket could take you off on a date any time, any place, anywhere. But by the Full Moon on the 26th you'll wonder how you could have been so shallow.

Get involved in helping to organize a social event to restore your faith in human nature and one lover in particular. Alluring Venus comes to your rescue and transforms what you thought was a flirtatious fling into something deeper. The ball's in your court at the end of the month and only you can decide where to aim it. Sensuous kisses and a long weekend of sexual healing should help make up your mind.

December

The New Moon on the 12th makes you a force to be reckoned with. Your eyes are widened to the romantic games people are playing and how you could make those dynamics work for you. But it means finding the right place and the right man. You're usually a mega party animal – and this is the festive season. But you feel disillusioned about the same old social scene around the 15th. You want adventure or exotic venues where no-one knows you and you can practice your romantic 'game plan'. So think of those same old office parties more as a stage where you can play the role of High Priestess. Equip yourself with some great one-liners, laugh your contagious laugh and a dull office 'do' turns out to be sensational. Follow three simple rules: 1. Don't snog the boss; 2. Don't throw-up in public; 3. Leave all other inhibitions at home. Suddenly you realize how ridiculous it is to think you'd rather sit on the sidelines watching people make fools of themselves all night. It's time to put on your dancing shoes and play the seduction game, especially when a sensual stranger grins at you across the room. Shimmy and gyrate your body in perfect time to his and he'll be aching to touch you all over. By the time of the Full Moon on the 26th your mobile is full of this new rogue's sexy text messages. So knock a going-nowhere relationship on the head on the 29th and free yourself up for some more gyrations with your private dancer. Groove your hips together into the New Year – it looks like this could be one fated attraction that proves to be a wonderful destiny too.

Your Love
Horoscope
2004

Love
Compatibilities

Who's most likely to be Mr Right or simply Mr Right Now? Knowing who's compatible and who you might find hard work will give you insight into your own emotional, romantic and sexual needs too. Some zodiac signs might want romance or a 'no strings attached' relationship, others want marriage or a highly workable professional partnership. This very brief guide can give you some clues to who you might find a challenge, a push-over, a one-night wonder or simply the man of your dreams.

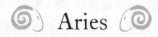 Aries

Aries woman/Aries man

Immediately a powerful rapport, but who's the boss? Both of you are impulsive and vain, so there could be a few arguments about who gets the bathroom first. You both leap hellbent into relationships, but neither of you bears any resentment towards the other if you part.

Aries woman/Taurus man

You enjoy a mutual fascination for your very differences. You admire his cooking skills, he's glad you prefer to be boss in bed. Luckily this means you can have sex all night and a gourmet dinner every evening. Together you'll have sex anywhere from a sauna to a bunk bed, but watch out he doesn't fall asleep just when you're ready for more.

Aries woman/Gemini man

You both experience physical bliss in this relationship and he's quickly aroused if you play out some of your sexual fantasies. You love his quick wit and restless spirit, but he's not so fond of being dominated. Incredibly stimulating for both of you, as long as you both give each other space.

Aries woman/Cancer man

Initially you're convinced he's ambitious and self-centred. This is only a cover-up – he doesn't want you to see his gentle side. Excellent for a short-term affair, but you may tire of his indirect way of dealing with life when you'd rather just get on with it.

Aries woman/Leo man

Expect to get on like a house on fire, to begin with anyway. You both need to dazzle and shine, but Leos tend to be ultra proud and your flirtatious sparkle may make him jealous. Good for a glamorous partnership, but not strong on intellectual rapport.

Aries woman/Virgo man

Together you are the most virtuoso performers imaginable. You enjoy a perfect sex life, but you have to be ready to match his performance and take his criticism. Both of you have little in common mentally or emotionally, but physically sparks can fly.

Aries woman/Libra man

This is often a combustible relationship, but always sexy and challenging. Your fiery approach to sex is both compelling yet threatening to his more aesthetic ideals about love – he needs beautiful surroundings and subtle provocation. Always fascinating and seldom forgettable.

Aries woman/Scorpio man

This man can be too intense and deep for your more dynamic and extrovert style. You'll enjoy an exhilarating sex life, but there's a danger he wants total commitment. Giving up your independence is unlikely, so be prepared for a long haul of emotional battles.

Aries woman/Sagittarius man

Could prove to be the biggest romantic thrill. Sex is just one big adventure once you've fallen into his arms, but heroes have a knack of disappearing at a moment's notice. Good for laughs and physical romps, but be prepared to cross canyons to find him.

Aries woman/Capricorn man

He may be more conventional than you about how your sexual relationship develops. You love taking risks and having fun, and initially he finds this totally mind-blowing. But he prefers the kind of risks that lead to business success rather than simply to bed.

Aries woman/Aquarius man

There's an interesting rapport here, with both of you needing oodles of freedom. He adores your impulsive nature but often prefers to observe life rather than get involved in it. Good for long conversations into the night. The only problem is you're hot and he's sometimes just too cool.

Aries woman/Pisces man

You both have totally different social needs. He wants to be everyone's friend, you don't. He's dreamy, elusive and often unpredictable, and you're flattered by his sensitivity to your sexual needs. He either falls hopelessly in love with you or runs a mile when he sees how volatile you are.

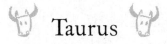# Taurus

Taurus woman/Aries man

An instant magnetism pulls you together. He is impatient, dashing and vain. You have to keep your cool and adore him for his sexy smile and good humour. Don't try to force him to make any commitments and he'll stick around longer than you'd imagine.

Taurus woman/Taurus man

You're likely to be spending most of your time on the horizontal. Both of you love sensual pleasure and both of you enjoy indulgence. There's lots of silent tenacity and mutual defiance out of the bedroom, but a wonderful earthy rapport as long as you both remember to communicate.

Taurus woman/Gemini man

You adore his ability to play any role you desire, both in and out of bed. But don't ever get possessive about him or he may disappear faster than he appeared. Good for romantic fun and erotic sex, but he's totally unreliable and utterly flirtatious with your friends.

Taurus woman/Cancer man

You both require tenderness and both need time to allow your sexual secrets to unfold. Your fantasy world intrigues him and his might take a lifetime to explore. Warmth and companionship are important to you both; your only test is when you both sulk for days over an upset.

Taurus woman/Leo man

There's oodles of sexy magic between you, but you have little in common emotionally. Both of you communicate in very different ways and are liable to stubborn moods. It's an incredibly strong relationship if you respect each other. He needs loyalty and to be treated like a king; you love sensually indulging him.

Taurus woman/Virgo man

Your earthy sensuality lifts him off to a different plane when he realizes you're the most perfect woman he's ever met. You might find him too clinical about sex and he might eventually decide you're too self-indulgent. Good for a long-term stability, but lacking in passion.

Taurus woman/Libra man

As long as you give him plenty of space to socialize he sticks around. But remember he lives in his head and doesn't like to be brought down to earth too often. Both of you like winding the other up in public, but in private you just like to laze around in each other's arms.

Taurus woman/Scorpio man

This is one of the most erotic combinations of the zodiac – you're sensual and steamy, he's torrid and sexually demanding. He's drawn to your earthy needs and you to his extremes of passion. A transformative relationship that can be total love or total hate.

Taurus woman/Sagittarius man

You could have problems. He's a rover and doesn't really want to be committed. If you're prepared for him to wander and return to your side when he feels like it, then you'll be rewarded with a fabulous lover and friend. Not easy for long-term commitment.

Taurus woman/Capricorn man

Once you establish a rapport with this man there's usually a strong bond between you. Sexually, you're more sensual than he is – you need tactile warmth, he usually prefers to be plotting business coups. Maybe it's time to teach him some new tricks? Good for long-term commitment.

Taurus woman/Aquarius man

Both of you are fascinated by your very different personalities. Aquarians love to be alone or with a million pals and need more freedom than anyone else. Good for a fun-loving affair, as long as you can tolerate his ex-lovers being his friends.

Taurus woman/Pisces man

You can get lost in his imaginative world and are fascinated by his sensitive nature and intuitive talents. He's far stronger than he appears on the surface and you're emotionally deeper than he realizes. Together you can establish a long-lasting instinctual rapport.

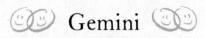 Gemini

Gemini woman/Aries man

Initially his crazy ideas bewitch you and you fall for his impulsive need for spur of the moment sex. There's a great physical rapport here, but he's too egotistic at times. It's a passionate but exhausting relationship. Intellectually he can't match you, so you may tire of him long before he tires of you.

Gemini woman/Taurus man

You are instantly attracted to his very feral masculinity. His body intrigues you and his sexual performance thrills you. However, he does love routine in his life and you prefer anything but that. Excellent if you want stability and constancy, not so good for variety and fun.

Gemini Woman/Gemini man

You're like a couple of identical twins. Intellectually stimulating and always buzzing, both of you are adventurous and on the look-out for new ideas. Good for mutual understanding, but you're both easily led astray by a beautiful face, so chances of instability high.

Gemini woman/Cancer man

This captivating rogue makes you feel cherished, for a while anyway. However, he's home-loving and possessive and you're extrovert, flirtatious and need space. Physically compelling, but difficult to sustain.

Gemini woman/Leo man

He's generous, warm and sincere and you adore his dramatic and fiery nature. However, you could find it hard to keep playing the role of the ultra glamorous celebrity. Great for sex, sex and more sex, but he can get too arrogant about his performance.

Gemini woman/Virgo man

You both feel an instant attraction or an instant repulsion. Intellectually he could assume you're not as clever as him and he's liable to criticize your every move. Could be fun for a crazy fling, but usually lacking in long-term mutual passion.

Gemini woman/Libra man

His idealistic, romantic nature bewitches you. Out and about you probably discuss the world, play mental games and enjoy romantic adventures. Good intellectual rapport, but he likes everything to be ultra perfect, so remember to wear beautiful lingerie and clean the bath.

Gemini woman/Scorpio man

Very different natures at work here, so often an erotic connection. Can be a complete love-hate drama. Sexually wild and often unpredictable, passionate and volatile. If you like leaping in at the deep end, then this is the man for you.

Gemini woman/Sagittarius man

You've met your match. Not only is he your opposite sign which means there's an extraordinarily powerful attraction between you, but also he's the most exciting lover. Passionate and heroic, he leaps into your life bringing adventure in his wake, but he can disappear equally as fast.

Gemini woman/Capricorn man

You're put on the spot and feel like you're being cross-examined. Not only do you feel restricted by his conventional attitude to life, but you also get impatient with his calculated plans. Physically worth pursuing purely out of Gemini curiosity, but unlikely to be a long-term affair.

Gemini woman/Aquarius man

Your mind fascinates him and he spends hours analyzing every inch of you. You quickly establish a genuine and permanent intellectual rapport. Can be an unpredictable but long-lasting relationship. Secret: he may prefer more sexual freedom than he's willing to admit.

Gemini woman/Pisces man

Here's a man who can adapt to your own changeable and restless nature. He drifts with your needs and indulges in your fantasies if you ask him. He's just as happy to talk through the night as he is to be utterly sensual.

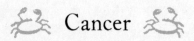

Cancer

Cancer woman/Aries man

He's drawn to your cool sensuality and you adore his fiery sexuality. His passion is naked; yours is clandestine and secret. Words like commitment and security send him running. Great for a fling and a wild passionate affair, but he's not interested in your feelings – he's only interested in himself.

Cancer woman/Taurus man

Both of you have a need for closeness, although his is more physical and yours more emotional. Together you can create a serene lifestyle because neither of you wants to score points over the other. Excellent for sexual pleasure and long-term happiness.

Cancer woman/Gemini man

He loves to talk about his sexiest fantasies, while you prefer to keep your sexual thoughts to yourself. His nature is geared towards variety and intellectual stimulation, while yours is towards feelings. Could be okay for a casual affair, but not easy if you want commitment.

Cancer woman/Cancer man

Both of you are equally evasive, especially about your private fears and desires. And both of you fear rejection more than anything else, so opening up to each other could take a long time. But physical happiness will be the most profound and magical of experiences if you do.

Cancer woman/Leo man

Flamboyant and impulsive, the Leo man's egotistic needs are very demanding. But you adore his protective attitude and he loves to be loved. If you can reveal your true warmth, he is utterly devoted. The only downside is his stubbornness and your evasiveness.

Cancer woman/Virgo man

Meticulous beyond belief, he believes that what you see is what you get, while you have mood swings and need to experience the mysteries in life. Both of you feel deeply but rarely open up to each other.

Cancer woman/Libra man

You respond eagerly to his idealistic vision of love and he adores your sensitive, sensual nature. But as you begin to slowly open up and reveal your feelings and changing moods, his airy, abstract approach to life may not rest comfortably with your emotional world.

Cancer woman/Scorpio man

Apparently the master of sexual pleasure, he's the most irresistible man you've ever met. But he won't be able to stop himself from wanting to own you. Good for an erotic, deeply emotional relationship, but take care, this man can destroy that which he loves.

Cancer woman/Sagittarius man

Because you have such different ways of looking at the world, a powerful magnetic attraction pulls you together. He adores your secretive side and you love his sparkling optimism. A creative relationship but short-lived. He wants freedom and a nomadic lifestyle; you need commitment and a nest.

Cancer woman/Capricorn man

You need to feel in control of your emotions and he needs to feel in control of his life. So you both play sexy games of one-upmanship to defend your vulnerable side. Your mysterious femininity keeps him hooked. An ambitious relationship, deeply satisfying and often long-lasting.

Cancer woman/Aquarius man

Different energies here – he needs detachment, you need closeness. He may make you feel sexually liberated, but once he's uncovered your secrets and told you about everything under the sun, he won't hang around for long.

Cancer woman/Pisces man

You both have an intuitive understanding of each other's feelings. He knows how to please you and you know what goes on behind his role-playing. A very private relationship, but one where you have to make the decisions if you're ever going to get out of the house or on to the next party.

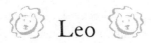 Leo

Leo woman/Aries man

He is impulsive and vain; you are always proud and uncompromising. Your fiery enthusiasm can burn itself out and there's always a danger of you both tiring of each other's competitive attitude to love. Great for fun flings, but long-term happiness can be difficult.

Leo woman/Taurus man

This man is a sensual artist, but he doesn't aspire to flamboyant behaviour. Great for physical fulfilment as long as he doesn't get a little frustrated by your desire for glamorous living and always acting the part of queen bee.

Leo woman/Gemini man

The big problem here is that he lives in his head and you live through your heart. When he's with you he's an entertaining prankster, but also a bit of a gangster. You want loyalty and probably this is the last man on earth to give it, especially when he'd rather be flirting with your friends.

Leo woman/Cancer man

He's moody and often silent; you're passionate, vibrant and glitzy. He's inspired by your fiery nature and need for complete honesty and loyalty. A love affair of passion – your only problem being his need to retreat when you'd rather be socializing every night.

Leo woman/Leo man

The passion you generate together could become a battleground of wills. You both have a natural desire to out-pleasure each other. Fiery and rampant, neither of you has time to consider making commitments. Highly compatible, if you can both remember to honour those hidden emotions.

Leo woman/Virgo man

Workable but not necessarily long-lasting. It is a very creative relationship as you respect each other's different approach to life.

But he could resent your constant need for glamorous socializing, while you might get fed up with having to be the cleaner.

Leo woman/Libra man

Both of you love to get out and about, look good and enjoy a glittering social scene, but his indecisiveness may eventually irritate you. Wonderful for sexual fun and to feel truly adored, but difficult to pin him down or make any long-term plans.

Leo woman/Scorpio man

This relationship is a battleground for two powers intent on their own emotional and physical fulfilment. You are showy, teasing and dynamic; he is smouldering, intensely serious and often difficult to satisfy. Don't flirt with anyone else and he could be yours for as long as you choose.

Leo woman/Sagittarius man

Dynamic and impulsive romance, but don't expect him to make commitments. This man prefers his freedom and he isn't terribly loyal when variety is at stake. Great for physical fun, but he's a roamer not a fixture and fitting.

Leo woman/Capricorn man

The rapport between you is exciting, dramatic and erotic, and this often makes for a steamy sensual relationship. He loves your outrageous sexual style; you adore his potent, earthy libido. A passionate and challenging relationship – your only problem is you both need to dominate in and out of the bedroom.

Leo woman/Aquarius man

He believes in non-exclusive relationships and you believe in utter exclusivity. You are proud and demanding; he's detached about his feelings and believes in universal love. An attraction of opposites which can succeed, but he's likely to stray if you get possessive.

Leo woman/Pisces man

A strangely rich and satisfying relationship in the beginning, where fantasy mixes with drama. He loves to be dominated but may find it hard to keep up with your passionate demands. Great for escape, romance and intrigue, difficult for long-term companionship.

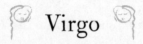 # Virgo

Virgo woman/Aries man

He's arousing and enticing, while you enchant him with your cool and classy charisma. Definitely an attraction of very different types, and it could be seriously romantic if you can accept his very extrovert needs and he can understand your need for privacy.

Virgo woman/Taurus man

This is one of the most potent and often long-lasting of zodiac relationships. He is practical, earthy and has similar sexual needs. He's a sensualist and you're a perfectionist, but together you can make a superb workable relationship.

Virgo woman/Gemini man

You adore his mischievous phone calls and witty one-liners. Both of you are mentally seductive. He warms quickly to your earthy sensuality but may prefer a more uncommitted relationship than you. Great for a laugh, difficult for long-term bliss.

Virgo woman/Cancer man

Immediately you feel comfortable in his very needy arms. You love being wanted, but his moods and unpredictability could be too disorganized for your methodical approach to life. An enriching rapport, but only long lasting if you let him close enough to your heart.

Virgo woman/Leo man

You easily relate to his high standards of beauty, sexual attraction and polished performance. But don't ever suggest he needs to make improvements – he believes he's already perfect. A warm sexy relationship if you've both got the patience.

Virgo woman/Virgo man

Here's a man who understands your basic earthy approach to life. But he probably won't awaken your passionate wild side. Great for trust, friendship and a working partnership, but ultimately not a dynamic relationship.

Virgo woman/Libra man

Physical and mental harmony for both of you. He's idealistic though and wants only the most complete romantic experience every time.

Both of you are gentle lovers and need refinement, but he's the real perfectionist, so make sure you never slip up.

Virgo woman/Scorpio man

You feel like you've been thrown in at the deep end. This man's magnetic sexuality is very intense. You're compelled into a deeply transformative relationship but may not be able to accept his need for domination. Great for a fling but remember he has a sting in his tail.

Virgo woman/Sagittarius man

He's a great sexual adventurer and usually loves to roam free, but he adores your feminine mystique and your cool earthy approach to life. Both of you are adaptable, so a relationship could prove highly exciting if you can tolerate his unreliability.

Virgo woman/Capricorn man

Together you enjoy a wonderful sexual rapport that relies also on a bond of companionship. Likely to be a seriously long-lasting involvement – he gives you that sense of stability and you keep him enchanted with your easygoing but materialistic approach to life.

Virgo woman/Aquarius man

A highly original and quite unusual relationship. He's fascinated by your sensible streak, you by his detached view of love and life. However, this is a relationship based on intellectual rapport rather than a deeply potent one. Great if you want a truly loving friendship.

Virgo woman/Pisces man

A wonderful sexual rapport – you take pleasure in his very intuitive romantic style, while he adores your earthy sensuality. Both of you can adapt to the other and you enjoy a deeply-connected sexual and emotional relationship. Often long-lasting.

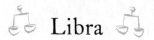

Libra

Libra woman/Aries man

You've met your natural opposite and like any polarity this could be a knockout relationship. You're romantic and idealistic and this man usually fulfils most of your dreams. He loves to be in charge; you adore having decisions made for you.

Libra woman/Taurus man

His practical approach may not gel with your image of an ideal heroic lover and your need to be mentally amused could be frustrated by his desire for the facts. But together you can make a pretty good double act because you both love the beautiful things of life.

Libra woman/Gemini man

You're at home with his sexy and hilarious mind. He's not too emotionally intense and you're both adaptable enough to keep the relationship light and free-spirited. Great for fun and romantic sex, as long as you keep him amused.

Libra woman/Cancer man

An unusual blend of sexual spice and mystical attraction, both of you are enchanted by each other's different way of perceiving the world. Excellent long-term rapport, but you might just find his moodiness hard to handle.

Libra woman/Leo man

Both of you enjoy pleasure for the sake of pleasure, as long as it's mingled with compassion and love. He adores glamour; you love playing the part. Good sexual companionship and usually long-lasting and sparkling.

Libra woman/Virgo man

Together you physically and emotionally understand one another and your quest for an ideal could end with him. Your only problem is that he can accuse you of all kinds of faults and flaws when in fact he's actually not that perfect himself.

Libra woman/Libra man

There's an instant rapport between you, simply because you are so similar. You both have an aura of romantic tenderness and adore all kinds of sexy fantasies, thoughts and games. A harmonious affinity, but only if one of you makes all the decisions.

Libra woman/Scorpio man

You fall into a very deep and intense sexual relationship, bewitching each other with your very differences. It's intensely passionate, but you might feel at times you want more space and a decent social life, while he wants to draw the curtains and be alone with you.

Libra woman/Sagittarius man

As long as you can keep up with his roaming lifestyle this is a fun relationship. He needs independence but also loves to be loved for who he is, so give him loads of space and he'll be back for more. Sexually exciting, with few emotional storms.

Libra woman/Capricorn man

He has a very different approach to sex and life from you. He thrives on straightforward, earthy, no-nonsense relationships – you prefer the romantic. Excellent as a discrete fling, but long-term there could be power struggles about money and property.

Libra woman/Aquarius man

You enjoy a fantastic physical rapport based on mental games. However, he's more fascinated by your mind than your body and his independent lifestyle may conflict with your need for a constant companion. Wonderful for a fun-loving, easy-going relationship.

Libra woman/Pisces man

Escape into a land of romantic fantasy. You enjoy an instant sexual rapport and often it's a successful relationship. He is looking for the ultimate experience and you're looking for the perfect one. But imagination may not be enough to keep you together when good old reality kicks in.

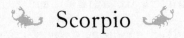 Scorpio

Scorpio woman/Aries man

Assured of physical action, you have dynamic fun wherever you go. He's challenging and impulsive but has a very different nature from your own. Your possessiveness could push him to the limits and his need for independence could leave you lonely.

Scorpio woman/Taurus man

Taurus is your natural opposite in the zodiac and this means the tension between you will be like a magnet – this is a love or hate relationship in the extreme. You hold an erotic fascination for each other which is often long-lived but can be exhausting, possessive and emotionally challenging.

Scorpio woman/Gemini man

You want to plummet into the depths of his amusing, ambiguous personality. He needs constant variety and is fascinated by your secret side. However, he avoids emotional intensity, whereas you prefer exclusive closeness. Great for mental games, difficult for long-term rapport.

Scorpio woman/Cancer man

Fascinated by one another's very private nature, you both crave complete physical and emotional closeness, and together are assured of dedicated companionship. Good relationship potential, but he may not be as passionate and as wild as you might secretly have hoped for.

Scorpio woman/Leo man

Although for a while you're happy to play his games, your need for a serious physical involvement could alarm him. Both of you are demanding and enjoy challenging the other, but his line-up of glamorous friends and exes may make you jealous.

Scorpio woman/Virgo man

Needing an earthy and ordered love life, he's discriminating and laid-back. You, on the other hand, have a more passionate, chaotic approach to relationships and could feel emotionally unfulfilled. Especially as he prefers to keep a big distance from his own feelings.

Scorpio woman/Libra man

He craves the perfect relationship and loves being subjected to your intense mystical power. You both enjoy his fantasy world and have a great sexual rapport, but you both have very different needs and desires. You want all or nothing; he wants to be free and easy.

Scorpio woman/Scorpio Man

There's an instant affinity between you, both sexually and emotionally, but you could both end up playing too many power games. Exciting and intense, but often too stormy too soon, unless you truly enjoy the danger element of who can outwit the other first. Sexy and wicked.

Scorpio woman/Sagittarius man

You're attracted to his opportunist nature, but his fiery spirit doesn't involve feelings. He needs to be free to come and go as he pleases, whereas you need to know exactly where and what he's doing. Sexually exciting and great for a fling, but could be a very steamy, torrid affair.

Scorpio woman/Capricorn man

Both of you are aroused by power and there could be some fascinating conflicts surrounding your mutual need to be in control. He learns from your intense passion for life and you from his pragmatic one.

Scorpio woman/Aquarius man

This is a highly magnetic and erotic relationship. But you want total involvement, he doesn't. The main problem is that his freedom means more to him than you do. Great for an unconventional relationship, if you can defuse your jealous streak.

Scorpio woman/Pisces man

You enjoy a sensual rapport, but this relationship is highly challenging. He's a social animal and prefers to roam his social circle telling everyone about you. You're discrete and don't want your intimate life broadcast around town. Good for sexual affinity, but lifestyle needs are very different.

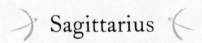

Sagittarius

Sagittarius woman/Aries man

This is a sexually exciting and passionate relationship, but when the flames die down, what's left? Probably the desire to go your own way. A fun-loving, challenging relationship, but difficult long-term as you both have very strong views about living independently.

Sagittarius woman/Taurus man

Strangely, can be extremely satisfying, as he's down-to-earth and very sexy with it. As long as he doesn't get too possessive, a long-term rapport can develop. Simply because you need to feel there's always someone reliable around.

Sagittarius woman/Gemini man

You're natural opposites in the zodiac, so there's bound to be fireworks. You enjoy a magnetic sexual attraction, where your sex life is usually fast-paced and furious. Long-term this can work, as long as you accept that he looks at the bigger picture of life, while you want to work on the details.

Sagittarius woman/Cancer man

Hmm. He's home-loving, but you're not exactly fond of leaning over a hot stove more than you can help. But he comes up trumps if he agrees to be the domestic saint while you get on with your hi-flying career. Sexually inspiring, but don't forget he's looking for a mother figure.

Sagittarius woman/Leo man

Daring, risky and often drawn together through your social scene, you both enjoy glamorous parties and flirting with everyone. Great for your image, but often doomed to separation, as you're both likely to get led astray by a gorgeous face.

Sagittarius woman/Virgo man

He can be enchanting enough to keep you guessing and has the sense of humour to put up with all your jokes. But he needs punctual dates and the same old friends. You prefer the unknown, the surprising and being late. Great for a sexy fling, difficult for long-term togetherness.

Sagittarius woman/Libra man

You're an utterly romantic duo when you first get together. And you feel as if you've finally met the man of your dreams. But take care when he starts saying 'we' at every possible moment, while you'd rather be saying 'I'. Great for sex and romance. Only long-term if you're willing to make compromises.

Sagittarius woman/Scorpio man

A very steamy relationship. He's compelling, sexually potent and irresistible, but he likes to be in control of the relationship, so watch out because he's jealous and provocative himself. 'Power play' likely, but physically breathtaking.

Sagittarius woman/Sagittarius man

You're drawn to each other because you see the best of yourself in each other's eyes. Can be a very long-term duet, but take care as you're both capable of being led astray after the initial fire has died down. Neither of you can have your cake and eat it, as you're both very jealous underneath that bravado.

Sagittarius woman/Capricorn man

Physically competitive, you're driven to out-seduce this man. But he's after conventional love and wants his woman – yes, remember those words, 'his woman' – to be the perfect business partner/caterer or career-seeker. You can handle the latter, but he won't be able to deal with your flirtatious side for long.

Sagittarius woman/Aquarius man

Excellent for a free and easy, 'no strings attached' relationship. You both need oodles of space and both avoid heavy-duty emotional scenes. A good friendship rather than a passionate torrid love affair, but isn't that actually quite refreshing?

Sagittarius woman/Pisces man

Sexy sparks abound. But he's even more elusive and unreliable than you are, so you keep missing each other on those last-minute impulsive dates. Great for romantic fun, difficult for anything which requires commitment or decision making.

Capricorn

Capricorn woman/Aries man

A battle of wills, but a very physical magnetism between you. But he needs a woman to hang on his arm like a gold chain. Great for a professionally successful partnership with loads of sex thrown in. Not high on romance or peace and quiet.

Capricorn woman/Taurus man

Materially, physically and mentally you're in tune, but, and there is a but, you could end up in more fights than you imagine simply because you can both get fanatical about your beliefs. Great sexual rapport – just take care who's in control of the credit card.

Capricorn woman/Gemini man

Steamingly sexy to begin with, but he's a man who needs constant change in his life or boredom immediately sets in. Then he's off flirting the night away while you're doing the ironing. Not easy long-term, but could be a laugh a minute while he's enthusiastic and kept amused.

Capricorn woman/Cancer man

You're opposites of the zodiac so you're drawn to each other like moths to each other's flames. This is a very sexy, extremely serious relationship and often it's successful in the long-term. It's better if you're both ambitious to reach the top of your profession.

Capricorn woman/Leo man

A glamorous liaison built on a mutual desire for wealth or ambition. But he's very vain, so make sure you always treat him as if he were the only man on earth. Your only problem is that you can get tired of his self-righteous streak.

Capricorn woman/Virgo man

Stability is important for both of you, and as you're both Earth element signs, you have an affinity for the same pleasures in life. A sensually-fulfilling relationship, as long as he accepts your need to be in control and you can deal with his mercurial teasing side.

Capricorn woman/Libra man

Initially you're attracted by your very differences. He's romantic and idealistic, you're down-to-earth and want security. Long-term he might still hanker for the perfect woman, even though you know you're exactly that.

Capricorn woman/Scorpio man

This relationship is challenging and often highly successful. You're both driven by power and both prefer a very private relationship. But you're more of a social animal than he is and he could become resentful of your ambitious achievements if he's not one up on you. Sexually great, emotionally exhausting.

Capricorn woman/Sagittarius man

If you can put up with his need for freedom then he might hang around longer than you'd imagine. But he does admire success and anyone who name-drops. Status turns him on, so make sure you're aiming for celebrity acclaim, otherwise he'll be off on another scent once the initial passion's worn off.

Capricorn woman/Capricorn man

Sexy rapport, but although you both understand the other inside out, you always feel there's something missing. 'Power plays' and rivalry likely, so good for a challenging relationship. But it might be you who falls in love with a wild romantic or lone wolf while he's out making money for the sake of it.

Capricorn woman/Aquarius man

Strangely addictive. You both love the other because you're so different but will probably want each other to adapt to your own way of thinking. Can be a highly successful relationship if he accepts you need things done by the book and you accept he needs freedom to do whatever he likes.

Capricorn woman/Pisces man

His very changeable moods could mean you get a little hot under the collar. Not an easy rapport, as you want things to be black and white and he prefers a few grey areas. Especially when he disappears when you're supposed to be entertaining your business chums. Sexy, but usually short-term.

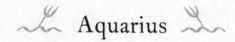

Aquarius

Aquarius woman/Aries man

Blazing with passion, he could be too physically direct for your more detached attitude to sex. But you adore shocking him with your sexual insights and flirting with his friends, and you send him erotic e-mails just to keep him on his toes. He's fiery and single-minded, you need independence. Watch out you don't burn each other out.

Aquarius woman/Taurus man

His physical passion is wild and untamed, but he does get incredibly fanatical about his possessions, which could include you. He may be too confining for your more detached, aloof lifestyle. An interesting experience, but rarely long-term.

Aquarius woman/Gemini man

You alternate between finding him totally stimulating and totally frustrating. But a good long-term relationship, as he's fascinated by your mind and you love his ability to give you the freedom you crave. Watch out for his flirtatious streak though.

Aquarius woman/Cancer man

Could be a good sexual relationship if he's prepared to accept friendship is more important to you than 'coupledom'. But he's a 'one-woman man' so the problem arises when your male friends pitch up for coffee and he realizes you're not exclusively his. Very sexy attraction, but not often long-term unless you want a 'man indoors'.

Aquarius woman/Leo man

He can offer you complete physical bliss, but he does require loyalty in return, which you may not be prepared to give to one man. He adores your independence and your wild, unconventional approach to sex. An exciting rapport as long as you accept his need for prestige.

Aquarius woman/Virgo man

Both of you avoid emotional involvement. You have stunningly different temperaments and therefore find each other very addictive, but you both might just forget to talk about your feelings and hurt one another unintentionally.

Aquarius woman/Libra man

This man's an idealist whose romantic sexuality could lead you deeply astray. A lively, fun-loving relationship with little emotional intensity, which suits you down to the ground. He needs romantic conversations and together you create a fascinating rapport.

Aquarius woman/Scorpio man

A powerful attraction of very different needs and desires. Both of you like to take control of the relationship. He wants to be the boss, but you just want to control those feelings. Magnetic and irresistible, you may find you have little choice but to fall into his arms.

Aquarius woman/Sagittarius man

This is one man who needs greater freedom and space than you. A highly-successful physical relationship. You give each other enough time to do your own thing, without feeling suspicious or jealous. Good for an exciting liaison and an utterly honest attitude to life.

Aquarius woman/Capricorn man

You both have very different physical needs, as he needs a conventional lifestyle and you prefer anything but. Can be a lively, demanding and ambitious relationship, as long as he gives you your space and you give him the time of day in the first place.

Aquarius woman/Aquarius man

You share a natural affinity for the same physical and mental pleasures. Both of you approach relationships with a very open mind and experiment with taboo ideas. A great relationship – not deeply passionate but completely honest and mutually creative.

Aquarius woman/Pisces man

This man needs unconditional space, but he is still a romantic cleverly disguised as a pleasure-seeker. He's likely to become addicted to you, so watch out if you want complete freedom as he's so sensitive. Excellent for a romantic fling, but exhausting for anything long-term.

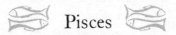 Pisces

Pisces woman/Aries man

Brimming with passion and audacity, he can't resist your lush sensuality and you easily surrender to his uninhibited sexual style. Difficult for a long-term relationship as you need to feel totally part of his pack, while he's a lone wolf.

Pisces woman/Taurus man

He won't understand the depths of your mysterious vulnerability but he treasures your sensitivity. You might persuade him to save a few whales, but he could be just too interested in making money to be charitable all the time.

Pisces woman/Gemini man

Both of you have ambivalent natures. At times he wants sexual fun filled with laughter, conversation and wine, and at others he disappears from your bed at dawn when he's on a mission. Enjoy those mind games, but you could get resentful when your fantasy world seems to be wasted on him.

Pisces woman/Cancer man

You're inspired by his sensual rhythms and varying moods of passion. There's a great sexual balance between you. He adores your femininity and your willingness to adapt to his unpredictable streak. The only problem is his need to be mothered – and yours to have a hero.

Pisces woman/Leo man

He's mesmerizing and you may feel like a princess, but he does need to know you'll be there for him on permanent standby. You prefer to escape into your dream world, he'd rather he was the only fantasy you had. Superb sexual rapport, but real life is difficult.

Pisces woman/Virgo man

This relationship provides a great contrast between perfection and sensual beauty. Together you have tense and testing moments. The sexual arousal between you is profound and you can develop a haunting devotion to one another. The only problem is you want to escape reality and he likes to be part of it.

Pisces woman/Libra man

A very romantic kick-off, but his intellectual approach to life and love may begin to disturb you when you'd rather be drifting on the tide without a care in the world. A dreamy, almost unreal relationship, but sexually irresistible.

Pisces woman/Scorpio man

Excellent for a sexual fling, but you get defensive when he thinks he owns you. If he gives you enough space, then long-term prospects are good, but he'll have to accept your flirtatious streak. This is Mr Jealousy, don't forget.

Pisces woman/Sagittarius man

He's a bit of a sexual roamer, while you're interested in clandestine romance, so you might meet through a love triangle. He could prove to be the most exciting lover you've ever met. You enjoy a wonderful sexual rapport as long as you give each other space.

Pisces woman/Capricorn man

Preferring to keep his own feelings locked away, you may find his physical needs are just not enough to keep you deeply involved. You fall under his dominant spell, but not an easy long-term relationship.

Pisces woman/Aquarius man

His radical belief system may jar with your more ephemeral ideals and although physically it's all very arousing, there could be difficulties in the rhythm of your very different emotional make-up. Good for a short-term fling or affair.

Pisces woman/Pisces man

Because you are so similar you play the same games, changing the rules when one fears rejection from the other. Trapped in a mutual fantasy world, neither of you are interested in the reality. Totally erotic, but your dependency on one another may result in one of you acting the martyr through fear of abandonment.

A Final Word

For further information about Sarah, visit her web site:

http://www.sarahbartlett.com

Fated Attraction

Your Complete Zodiac Guide to Seduction

Sarah Bartlett

This scintillating and accessible book is for every woman in love, and those still looking for the man of their dreams.

This is the book you and your friends will rush to consult as soon as you've met that new man. Now you can have the same kind of revealing and accurate compatibility reading usually available from a professional astrologer. As well as revealing how and why you attract certain men to you, which men you fall for, which to avoid, and with whom you are most compatible, it also reveals the truth about the male psyche. Contents include:

- Attraction Factor
- Getting Personal
- Love Styles
- Chemistry Lesson
- Don't Take It Personally
- Game or Match?
- Creating Your Unique Compatibility Chart

Your Chinese Horoscope 2004

What the Year of the Monkey Holds in Store for You

Neil Somerville

The Year 2004 is the Chinese Year of the Monkey – what will this mean for you?

The ancient art of Chinese astrology, which predates the Western zodiac, has been in use in the Orient for thousands of years. The depth of its wisdom, and the accuracy of its detailed system of character analysis and prediction, has caught the imagination of the West in recent years and led to a rapid rise in its popularity. This complete astrological guide contains all the predictions you will need to take you into the year ahead – a year which offers great hope, advancement and opportunity.

This popular and enlightening guide, now in its sixteenth year, includes:

- An overview of the 12-year Chinese astrological cycle
- An introduction to the 12 animal signs of the Chinese zodiac
- An explanation of the Five Elements and which one governs your sign
- What the Year of the Monkey has in store for you, your family, your loved ones and friends

Neil Somerville is a well-established author in this field and one of the most popular writers in the West on Chinese horoscopes. His *Your Chinese Horoscope* guides have been translated into many languages around the world.

Your Personal Horoscope 2004

Month-by-Month Forecast for Every Sign

Joseph Polansky

This popular one-volume guide, now in its eleventh year, contains all you need to know about your personal horoscope for 2004. Be prepared for the future by reading these predictions for your year ahead and discover how you, your family, friends and lovers will fare. This book contains:

- A personality profile for each sign
- The year's forecast for 2004 – what you can expect in terms of wealth, home, social and love life
- A month-by-month forecast of your best days, worst days and the ideal days for you to attract love or money

Joseph Polansky is a leading US astrologer who has been practising astrology for over 20 years.

Make
www.thorsonselement.com
your online sanctuary

Get online information, inspiration and
guidance to help you on the path to physical
and spiritual well-being. Drawing on the integrity
and vision of our authors and titles, and with
health advice, articles, astrology, tarot, a
meditation zone, author interviews and events
listings, www.thorsonselement.com is a great
alternative to help create space and peace
in our lives.

So if you've always wondered about practising
yoga, following an allergy-free diet, using the
tarot or getting a life coach, we can point you
in the right direction.

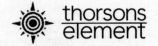
thorsons
element